r

Starting Out, Starting Over

FINDING
THE WORK
THAT'S WAITING FOR YOU

Linda Peterson

DB DAVIES-BLACK PUBLISHING • PALO ALTO

A NEW CENTURY COMMUNICATIONS BOOK

This book is dedicated to my mother, Helen Coury,
who has made it her career to always
be encouraging and supportive of my work.

Published by Davies-Black, a division of Consulting Psychologists
Press, Inc., 3803 E. Bayshore Road, Palo Alto, CA 94303. 1-800-624-1765.

99 98 97 96 95   10 9 8 7 6 5 4 3 2 1
Printed in the United States of America
Printed on recycled paper

Library of Congress Cataloging-in-Publication Data
Peterson, Linda
        Starting out, starting over : finding the work that's waiting for
    you / Linda Peterson. -- 1st ed.
            p.   cm.
        "A New Century Communications book."
        Includes index.
        ISBN 0-89106-073-1
        1. Vocational guidance.   2. Career changes.   I. Title.
    HF5381.P478   1995   95-4177
    331.7' 02--dc20   CIP

A New Century Communications Book

First edition
    First printing 1995

What's in This Book

Foreword

MY SIX-YEAR-OLD DAUGHTER wants to be a horse trainer. My seven-and-a-half-year-old son has decided that being a paramedic is his calling. How did they arrive at their decisions? Most probably it was their exposure to people who were doing those jobs. My daughter chose her future career after spending long hours at a barn with her teenage babysitter and her horse; my son witnessed firsthand the role that paramedics can play in helping an injured person get medical treatment and is a big fan of the TV show *Rescue 911.*

They'll no doubt change their minds dozens of times before they have to look for their first job. And that's fine and well. If we don't take the time to mentally "try on" different professions, we will probably end up in one by accident. And the chances of that career being right are as likely as hitting the jackpot in Las Vegas.

For most people, choosing a career is a winnowing down process; there are not dozens, but thousands of professions to consider. And unlike workers of a generation ago, today's employees are not only more aware of their career options, but are also more likely to have the mobility and access to education and training to pursue them.

Identifying which careers may be good matches, however, remains an unscientific and confusing prospect for most people. Those who have used assessment instruments such as the *Strong Interest Inventory* (*Strong*) and the *Myers-Briggs Type Indicator* (MBTI®) are fortunate because they have a jump-start on the process. Two chapters in this book will explain why.

When Consulting Psychologists Press was developing a new version of the *Strong,* one of the most respected and established assessment instruments of its kind, they decided it was time to introduce a book that would be a resource both for the professionals who administer the instrument and the people who take it. For the latter, it's a "where do I go next?" tool that is easy to read and act on. (The revised *Strong* was launched in late 1994.) They asked me to develop a framework for the book, one that would appeal to those who had taken the *Strong* as well as those who were unfamiliar with it but who were trying to decide on a career.

Acting as the architect of a book is one of the main tasks of a book producer, and I tackled this one with relish. Having written about job hunting and careers for over twenty years as a career editor (at *Glamour* magazine), a job columnist (for *New Woman, The New York Daily News, The Oakland Tribune,* and *The Boston Herald*), a career book reviewer (for *The Atlanta Journal-Constitution*), and an author (*The 90-Minute Résumé* and *Making It On Your First Job When You're Young, Ambitious and Inexperienced*), I was well-acquainted with the impact such an approach could have on the thousands of people who are still searching for meaningful career guidance.

Although there are many good career and job-hunting titles in bookstores, I have not found one that offers a realistic framework, in terms of time and effort, for making a smart career decision. I drafted the outline for *Starting Out, Starting Over* with that in mind. Author Linda Peterson interviewed numerous career experts, librarians, and career transition specialists to ensure that the decision-making models and the latest information-gathering methods, including the escalating volume of online services, were included in this book.

If you are flipping through the pages of *Starting Out, Starting Over*, I hope you will continue reading. Because what we—the author, the publisher, and I— have attempted to do is to give you a wonderfully detailed but easy-to-follow set of operating instructions on how to choose a career that will be satisfying to you based on its fit with your interests, personality, and values.

—Peggy Schmidt

Acknowledgments

THIS BOOK OWES most of its contents to the various contributions—large and small—of many caring and interested people. They include the following:

JoAnn Kroll, Bowling Green State University

Nancy Pool Dixson and Linda Evans, University of Denver

Carol Ellin, Goucher College

Ilene Rudman, Radcliffe Career Services

Marcia Fox and John Artise, Drake Beam Morin

George M. Needham, Public Library Association

Steve Oserman, Skokie Public Library

Georgia Donati, Mid-Manhattan Library Job Information Center, New York Public Library

Jacqui Anderson, Larchmont Public Library

Polly Hutcheson, National Commission for Cooperative Education

Susan H. Eubanks, National Board for Certified Counselors

Neale Baxter and Michelle Green, *Occupational Outlook Quarterly*

Linda Kuhns, U.S. Department of Labor

Larry Krumenaker, Mercury Information Services

Marilyn Moats Kennedy, Career Strategies

Janet Attard, Barbara Byro, and Vivian Kelly, GEnie

Jane Torbica, CompuServe

Tony Morelli and Elaine Hulbert, Prodigy

Frank Dobisky, Dobisky Associates

Maureen Carrig, Information Access Company

Mike Snodgrass, UMI

Nick Sparkman, COMSET

Alfred Glossbrenner

Jean M. Kummerow, Ph.D.

Pat Loban

Gerald M. Sturman, Ph.D.

Catharine Henningsen

Michele Jackman, American Association

Special acknowledgment to two experts at Info-PLACE, a service of the Cuyahoga County Public Library System in Maple Heights, Ohio: manager and career counselor Martin E. Jaffe, and librarian Kathleen M. Savage, a recognized authority on career materials. Both were very generous with their time and resources.

Thanks for her advice and encouragement to Elaine M. Sozzi, director of the WEBS Career and Educational Counseling Service of the Westchester Library System in Elmsford, New York.

Special thanks also to Federation Employment and Guidance Service (FEGS), a nonprofit human services agency in New York City. Steven Feldman, Ed.D., vice president of FEGS' Education and Career Services, made available two top resources: career counselors Judith Kelso, of FEGS' Career Development Services, and Barry Lustig, director of FEGS' Career Assessment Institute. For inquiries about FEGS' programs for counseling professionals or individuals seeking career guidance, contact FEGS at 235 Park Avenue South, 8th Floor, New York, NY 10003, or call 212-366-8481.

Finally, my thanks to the producer of this book, Peggy Schmidt of New Century Communications, for her unflagging cheer, encouragement, and vision.

Is This Book For You?

ON MONDAY MORNING, when the alarm clock buzzes you awake at 6:15, do you wish you were a VCR so you could fast-forward yourself to Friday night at five?

Have you been mentally drifting away so often at work that your colleagues are now prefacing their remarks to you with, "Earth to Larry!"?

If you're about to graduate from college and arc worried about your prospects, do you feel you had better accept any job that's offered and be grateful that you got it?

If any of these scenarios describe you, it's likely that you're among the unfortunate *majority* of workers who feel they're in the wrong job. As Richard Nelson Bolles, author of the famed *What Color Is Your Parachute,* concludes, "Huge life-decisions often are made in the whim of a moment. No wonder surveys of worker dissatisfaction find that up to 80 percent, or four out of every five workers, are dissatisfied with some important aspects of their jobs or careers."

The premise behind this book is that many of you have not yet accurately defined your right career. This can be true whether you're just starting out or once again are starting over with perhaps another unfulfilling job. Maybe you're reading this now because you've been forced to consider other options after being

▼ ▼ ▼ ▼ ▼ ▼ ▼

*Instead of asking,
who's hiring?,
the first question
should be:
Who am I?*

downsized out of your job. Maybe you fell into your work because of parental expectations or because you wanted to help in the family business, or even because someone in high school or college once told you that you were good with numbers and encouraged you to consider accounting. They were the "experts," and so you did what they suggested. But here you are...perhaps five, ten, or twenty years later, and you can no longer push aside your deep discontent. You have finally realized that it is time for a change.

This book is a career guide both for recent college graduates who are without direction and the career changers and explorers who perhaps for the first time are asking themselves what they really *want* to do. Many career seekers have in essence put the cart before the horse. Instead of asking, who's hiring?, the first question should be: Who am I? Self-assessment, not the job classifieds, is the first step in finding the work that's waiting for you—the work that's right for you.

The very nature of today's job market predicts that regular reassessment of what you can do will be the norm. In the workplace today, the only constant is change. Indeed, the latest guideline being used by career experts is that most people entering the workforce today will have three to five careers and eight to ten jobs. You need to develop what Charles Handy, management consultant and authority on the changing workplace, called a "skills portfolio"—the means by which you can reinvent and market yourself as you move through those careers. Flexibility and adaptability are key, and the need to keep learning is not going to stop once you land a job. You—not your current employer or your next employer—have the responsibility for your career development.

So in this rapidly changing workworld, you must know what you have to offer potential employers. What can you contribute to an organization? If you can't define that value, you are at a major disadvantage. The definitions you're looking for can be found in self-assessment.

What can this book offer career seekers—either first-timers or career changers? There are thoughtful exercises to aid in your self-assessment, practical guides to getting solid information—in print, in person, and in cyberspace—about the careers you're considering, and tools to help you in making your decision. This approach should give you a sense of whether you are ready to begin a job search, need additional training to enter a new occupation, or are actually happy doing what you're doing—either where you are or someplace else.

Above all, the intention is to offer you a career decision-making *process* that you can use again, when you are once more considering the next step in your worklife. In short, there is plenty of hands-on help here. Career counselors around the country were interviewed for their thoughts on career exploration today, and all were generous with their advice and glad to offer a little help. They know what you're going through.

To that end, one catalyst behind this book is the latest revision of the *Strong Interest Inventory* (*Strong*), a tool that has been helping career seekers for more than sixty years. It is a valuable assessment tool, one that anyone making a career decision should know about. Its equivalent on the personality front is the *Myers-Briggs Type Indicator* (MBTI) inventory, which provides insights about your personality and preferred style of dealing with the world and the workplace. Many who take it feel it provides a certain "aha" factor of enlightenment and self-understanding. The purpose of both instruments (which must be administered and interpreted for you by qualified professionals) and how they can help in the career exploration process are explained in detail in chapters 2 and 3. So

▼ ▼ ▼ ▼ ▼ ▼ ▼

*No book,
no workshop,
no counselor
can give you
"the answer"—
that can only
come from you.*

an assumption is being made in this book: that you will at some point take the *Strong* and the MBTI inventory as part of your self-assessment. These respected instruments can give you valid information and a sense of direction in your career search.

Career decision making is difficult for most people, and at some point you may find it helpful to spend a few sessions with a career counselor. Or maybe a career change workshop at a library or one of the local job hunter support groups sponsored by churches and service organizations will be the ticket to help you with the steps you are taking and the choices you are making.

But know this upfront: No book, no workshop, no counselor can give you "the answer." That can only come from you. As one library's handout readily acknowledges: "Ninety-nine and 44-one-hundredths percent of participants in our career decision workshop do not stand up at the end of the last session and say, 'Eureka! I have identified the perfect career for me and will look for a job tomorrow!'" But all these aids can help you begin to set goals and define your purpose.

As the author of a book on career decision making, I should note that I have always been interested in the ways people earn their livings and how they become involved with what they do. Or, in some cases, why they keep doing it, especially when they seem unsuited for it or are even openly miserable.

In that respect, I have never forgotten one of my summer jobs during college. I'd taken the civil service exam and was doing clerical work for a federal service agency. It was my first daily exposure to the high-rise building, white-collar world of work.

It was a world governed by the clock. The day promptly began at 8:15 A.M., and all employees had better be at their desks—tardy arrivals had to go sign the "late book," directly in front of the supervisor's glaring view. Everything in that office was done by the book: No one ever ventured outside of their job description or did anything they weren't required to do.

So I guess it should not have been surprising to me, given their dronelike existence, that the workers were always eager to go home, though eager is an understatement. As the minute hand on the huge clock above the main door lurched toward quitting time, this is what took place at the end of many a day: All the employees literally leaned forward on the edge of their chairs—clutching their coats and belongings, shoulders tensed, eyes glued to the clock—until they rose as one and dashed to the door as 4:59 P.M. ticked to 5:00. No one was left in the cavernous room by 5:01.

For a time, I was a bit amused by this performance, but, ultimately, I was a little saddened by it. I was only there for the summer; I knew I was "getting out." But here were all these people who clearly disliked what they did for a living—or at least the way it was done there—and for whatever reason, couldn't or wouldn't leave. I never dared ask why. But I went back to school remembering them, and I wondered...what must it be like to get up every morning dreading the workday ahead?

The point, then and now: You spend more waking hours on the job than doing anything else in your life. Work is not just a way to kill time until retirement; it's what you *do* with your life.

It would be nice if you enjoyed it.

The goal of this book is to help you start to define what that enjoyable work might be.

Making a Career Choice: An Overview of the Process

AN ACQUAINTANCE CALLS YOU UP and reports that his company is cutting 300 jobs, and his is one of them. "What exactly are you looking for?" you ask him. "Oh, I don't know...I'm open to suggestions," he replies. "I guess I'd like to try something different."

That fellow has a bigger problem than just being out of work. If *he* doesn't know what he wants and what he can do, how can anybody else help him find it? Jobs go to people who have the light of conviction shining in their eyes, not those who are "open to suggestions." But our friend is certainly not alone in his haphazard approach to finding another occupation.

People who are choosing their first career or changing their current one are often confused or even overwhelmed, and they blame it on the complexity and uncertainty in today's job market. But very often, they don't really know what they want because they've overlooked the critical first step: They don't really know who they are.

The content in this chapter was provided by career counselors Barry Lustig and Judith Kelso of FEGS, the Federation Employment and Guidance Service in New York City. Kelso is affiliated with FEGS' Career Development Services, which provides counseling and assessment to individuals. Lustig is director of FEGS' Career Assessment Institute, which offers consulting, training, and assessment services to corporate clients and counseling professionals.

1

Career counselor Barry Lustig, director of the Federation Employment and Guidance Service's (FEGS) Career Assessment Institute, notes that his agency's clients often are initially asked to cite what they consider to be their greatest strengths—the average person fizzles out within thirty seconds. Many of them have a very limited self-awareness and don't know what to say. Ideally, Lustig says, they should be able to speak about themselves, their skills, and their value to an organization for about three minutes. (Just consider the typical job interview question: "So, tell me about yourself. Why do you want to work for our company?")

Any decision is only as good as the information you base it on. So the first question in making a career decision is: What kind of person are you? When you know the answer, you can translate it to identifying the work that will satisfy the *skills* you want to use, your *interests,* your work *values,* and your *needs.* You find that answer through self-assessment.

You want to be able to say, I am the kind of person who...so I need to be in a career that.... For example, "I'm the kind of person who enjoys being creative, so I need to be in a career that allows much self-expression and is not highly structured." Or, "I'm the kind of person who gets a great deal of satisfaction from feeling needed, so I have to be in a career that helps other people." That kind of statement only comes from self-knowledge, but most career seekers don't have that information about themselves because they never asked themselves the right questions.

Let's say you're currently working as a paralegal and are thinking about becoming an attorney. After all, it seems logical enough—you're already in the legal field, right? But simply making the mental leap from being a paralegal to a lawyer based on your exposure to a law office is not a solid enough base for your decision.

First of all, you're not "a paralegal"—that's just your job title. That's what you list on your IRS form, and it's just one of many kinds of work you might do. Yet most of us label ourselves in terms of our job titles because we don't have a complete view of who we are. This stems partly from a societal pressure tied to our work identity. It's common to hear that people who have lost their jobs avoid going to parties or other social functions because they dread being asked that question, What do you *do*? The implication is that if you're not working, if you don't have a job title, then who *are* you? It should be obvious how limiting that is, because you're the same person, whether you're employed or not.

So you are not your job title. What you are is a unique combination of personality traits and skills and values and interests and needs and motivations.

That's not to say that once you know who you are and what you want that you can always manage to satisfy all your preferences on the job. Most career decisions today involve some tradeoffs in terms of your work values or the skills you want to use or your areas of interest; you seldom get everything you hope for met in a career. You will likely have to make compromises because of reality—both yours and the job market's. But the key thing is to have clarity about who you are apart from a job title. Then, based on that, you can begin to define and explore different options for yourself that might be a good fit.

How do you find what fits? Career decision making is based on both internal and external factors. The issue is merging your internal dynamics—your skills, interests, values, and personality—with the external realities of the world of work.

There are four stages in the career decision-making process:

1. Self-exploration
2. Occupational exploration
3. Goal setting and decision making
4. Implementation of the decision

▼ ▼ ▼ ▼ ▼ ▼ ▼ ▼

You are not your job title. What you are is a unique combination of personality traits and skills and values and interests and needs and motivations.

Each of these topics will be covered in depth in subsequent chapters. But first, it may be helpful to understand how each stage helps you to successfully accomplish your goal of choosing or changing your career.

Self-Exploration

This is the first and most important step—and the most critical to making a good career decision. Self-exploration gives you the answer to these questions: Who are you? What motivates you? What interests you? What skills and abilities do you most want to use? The process comes down to understanding your style, your skills, your motivation, and your developmental needs. Those variables are considered to be the most important factors relating to career success and satisfaction. Here's why.

STYLE

Simply put, your style is what comes naturally to you. It includes your personality and behavioral traits, and how you generally prefer to operate in the world, which is something that the *Myers-Briggs Type Indicator* (MBTI) inventory can tell you (see chapter 3). For example, part of your style in the workplace involves whether you like to work alone or as part of a team.

Knowing your natural style is a very positive way of looking at yourself, and it's critical to making a smart career choice. For example, if it does not come naturally to you to be aggressive, that's certainly not a deficiency. But those qualities are important in, say, many sales positions, and it would be helpful for you to know that certain sales careers would likely not be in sync with your style.

In the workplace, stress often occurs when you go against the grain—if you have to work in a way that is not consistent with your natural style.

SKILLS

People typically have a hard time identifying skills because they think of them in a very limited way. It's still not uncommon to hear a woman reentering the workforce after years as a homemaker say, "I've been at home for twelve years, so I really don't have any skills." No skills? Household management involves advising people, analyzing data, arranging social functions, budgeting expenses, coordinating travel and events, counseling people, handling complaints, finding information, listening to others, mediating disputes, operating equipment, setting agendas, planning and preparing meals, and keeping financial records.

Simply put, your skills are what you use to get things done. A skill has also been defined as anything that's goal oriented and can be improved with practice. In career decision making, it's most important to define the skill areas that you really enjoy using, the ones that energize you. You must know what you have to offer an employer now—your current skills—or what you want your skills to be, what you're willing to train or study to learn and develop.

There are three basic categories of skills: functional, adaptive, and work content, and we'll talk about each in some detail.

Functional Skills

These skills are often called *transferable,* meaning they can be used in a wide variety of work settings to do a wide variety of tasks. These are what you need to be able to pull out of your skills portfolio as you move and change throughout your worklife. They are usually described as your abilities in working with people,

> ▼ ▼ ▼ ▼ ▼ ▼ ▼ ▼
>
> *In career decision making, it's most important to define the skill areas that you really enjoy using, the ones that energize you.*

data, things, or ideas. Examples are organizing, writing, and analyzing.

Adaptive Skills

Also called *self-management* skills, these are your personal qualities and traits. People typically tend to minimize these "soft" skills and their importance, but they are very critical, especially in working with others. Adaptive skills such as patience and tactfulness directly affect the success of your relationships. Other examples are perseverance, tenacity, flexibility, attention to detail, and—especially in today's world of work—the ability to manage change.

Adaptive skills also are transferable, and the job market is increasingly going to make more demands on them. You can begin to define both sets of the above skills in chapter 4.

Work Content Skills

These are also referred to as *knowledge-based* or *job-specific* or technical skills. This is the information you possess about how to get something accomplished in a particular job, which may have little or no usefulness in another job. Work content skills are what you know about beekeeping or theatrical production or tax planning or training horses. It's knowing the jargon and techniques of a particular field.

By definition, since work content skills usually aren't transferable, they aren't as permanent a part of your skills portfolio as your adaptive and functional skills. However, they are vital for getting into a particular occupation and advancing if you choose to remain in it. Many job market experts say that today many employers want a person to be a combination of a generalist and a specialist, so work content skills can be very important. And there are always going to be new work content skills to learn—many jobs in the year 2000 will not even have existed ten years before.

MOTIVATION

This is a core dynamic—a composite of what drives you in the world. In short, what do you want to do and what don't you want to do? What kinds of activities charge your batteries? What makes you jump out of bed, eager to get to work on Monday mornings? Do you enjoy competing against others or just your own high standards? Do you always seek a new challenge or like the satisfaction of using a perfected skill?

Your motivation includes your career interest patterns, as indicated by the *Strong Interest Inventory* (*Strong*; see chapter 2), your work-related values, and your needs for such things as a certain degree of autonomy (see chapter 4). Your motivation is a major part of what could be called your *occupational self-concept,* based on your experience in the workplace so far and what you want it to be next. The combination of all these elements begin to form a pattern of what you really want out of your work. It should be easy to see that your satisfaction is going to increase if you are highly motivated in the work that you choose.

DEVELOPMENTAL NEEDS

To do a realistic self-assessment, it's not enough to know your strengths, you also need to identify your skill deficits that can impede your ability to do a particular job well. For example, the most common functional skills needing improvement are interpersonal skills—the ability to get along with others, create relationships, manage and influence people, and be a better listener. A work content deficit could be your need to develop computer literacy; an adaptive skill deficit could be your impatience.

These skill deficits or, to put a more positive spin on them, development needs, are usually things you can improve on once you're aware of them, either through training (work content skills) or by modifying your behavior. In chapter 4, you can define your most important adaptive skills and also note those you'd like to use that may need improvement. When you are aware of the "problem" adaptive traits, you can try to keep them from getting in your way.

For example, if one of your "positive" adaptive traits is that you're people oriented, your tendency may be to immediately say yes when someone at work asks for help. However, you may then become overwhelmed and stressed by the extra work you've taken on. But if you're aware that this can be a problem for you, you can employ a new strategy: When someone asks for assistance, don't feel you have to reply right away. Instead, you could say, "I'll get back to you on that, okay?" Then you can think it over and ask yourself if the assistance is something you are really able to give.

At this point, you may be thinking that this whole process of self-assessment sounds like a lot of time and effort and introspection, right? *It is.* But it's well worth your time now in terms of the payoff you'll enjoy in the future. The rewards of doing self-assessment are many. You can:

- *Build self-esteem and self-acceptance.* A person who has good self-esteem is able to say, I do certain things well and certain things not so well, but that's okay, that's who I am. It means having a balanced view of yourself. When it comes to knowing your strengths, your belief that you *can* do something directly affects your motivation to act. Unless you feel good about yourself, you may have difficulty moving forward. Indeed, having good self-esteem could be considered your most important adaptive skill.

- *Make a good career decision.* You need to believe that you have something to offer an employer in order to decide what you want to do. Because career choices are a function of the amount of information you have about yourself and the world of work, the new insights you derive will help you see how well you might relate to various careers and make the best choice.

- *Enhance your personal and professional effectiveness.* Are you good at managing time? stress? How efficient are you during the day? There's always room for improvement. In that respect, career development never stops. You always have to develop yourself, especially because of the flexibility and versatile roles the workplace demands today. Unfortunately, as career counselors point out, there's a phrase that fits many workers: "They have twenty years' experience, but it's really one year's experience repeated twenty times." In other words, there's been no real growth.

▼ ▼ ▼ ▼ ▼ ▼ ▼ ▼
Career development never stops. You always have to develop yourself, especially because of the flexibility and versatile roles the workplace demands today.

As stated earlier, self-exploration is the most critical step in the career decision-making process. The remaining stages, while important, will be dealt with more briefly here. Later chapters will provide you with the tools and resources you need to do the research and make decisions.

Occupational Exploration

This step involves investigating the world of work based on your knowledge of who you are. What specific jobs out there are most suitable for you at this stage of your life? Chapters 5 and 6 will show you how to research careers once you have identified your top choices.

There is a distinction between occupational exploration and job market exploration. The former describes the career and what it involves, while the latter is the reality of the labor market where you live or want to relocate to. (You will get the best and most up-to-date input on the job market when you do information interviews, discussed in chapter 7.)

Goal Setting and Decision Making

What do you need to know or do next to make the best career choice? This builds on your increasing self-awareness: From what you now understand about your values and preferences and needs, how can you begin to prioritize them? This step involves research to get the facts you need, learning what your career options are, and weighing how well each will satisfy your values and use the skills that are most important to you. This is also when you have to consider the realities of the job market—either where you are or where you want to be—and perhaps make compromises as you consider a decision. Chapter 8 discusses career decision making in detail.

Implementation of the Decision

A decision is only an intellectual exercise until you act on it. Once you've made a career choice, you usually take one of the following actions. If you already have the skills or knowledge required for the job you want, you prepare for the actual job search by shaping up your résumé, strategizing your job campaign, and networking for job leads. Or you start making plans to reality test your new choice (see chapter 9) and get the training or education you may need to get that job (see chapter 10).

Of course, all that sounds more straightforward than it actually is. Making a decision and then implementing it are not easy tasks. Obstacles can get in your way—and some of them may come from *you*. Problems called internal barriers can interfere with your taking action. These barriers include factors such as your perfectionism, fear of failure, ambivalence, and overall anxiety about the decision.

For example, if you're a perfectionist, you may second-guess yourself to death and doubt that you made or can make the right decision. Or if you can't decide among several career options, this may reflect ambivalence or fear of commitment: If you commit to one career, you obviously must give up something else.

Your anxiety can cause you to strive for what's called *premature closure*—meaning you try to make a fast career choice without enough self-assessment and occupational exploration, just because being undecided is so uncomfortable. But if you short circuit the self-awareness and research phase, you're shortchanging yourself.

Barry Lustig likes to use the following analogy regarding career decision making:

> Too many people don't know where they're going, but they're in a rush to get there. I say that people often want to take the express train instead of the local. But if they try to go too fast, they will miss several stations, and thus overlook what might be appropriate choices. Taking the express might get you to where you think you want to go faster, but when you do get off, it might be at the wrong stop.

It's important to note that there is a difference between indecision and indecisiveness. Indecision means you're having difficulty making a decision, mostly because you lack information either about yourself or the world of work. You generally make decisions pretty well; it's just that you don't have all the facts you need yet, say, in your occupational exploration. If you're provided with this information, you'll be able to move ahead and choose a plan of action.

Indecisiveness, on the other hand, means that you generally have difficulty making decisions; it's not just due to insufficient data but usually is more deep seated. In other words, if you were given sufficient information on which to base a decision, you would still have the same problem.

It can become a vicious cycle: When you're indecisive, you have difficulty taking action; and if you don't take action, it can get you depressed; and when you

▼ ▼ ▼ ▼ ▼ ▼ ▼ ▼

"Too many people don't know where they're going, but they're in a rush to get there. I say that people often want to take the express train instead of the local."

BARRY LUSTIG
CAREER COUNSELOR

feel bad about yourself, you don't move forward. If this scenario already has happened to you or you fear that it might, it can sometimes be dealt with by seeking some kind of support during the career selection process. This may mean simply talking it over with a friend or someone who's also going through the same thing, or getting help from a professional career counselor (see chapter 8). You have to take some steps—even small ones—to problem solve, to do something.

Sometimes people go to career counselors and say they're thinking of three different careers and can't decide because they want to know absolutely for sure that there's a "right" option. But in careers, as in life, you never know absolutely for sure about anything. All three careers may well be appropriate, but at some point you have to let go of two of them and *act*. A counselor will tell you—and you can tell yourself—that you must recognize that any decision you make will not be perfect.

You can't eliminate uncertainty, but you can minimize it. The best way to alleviate that anxiety is to know that you did your homework. There should be some measure of confidence in your ultimate decision if, to use the previous example, you know that you thoroughly investigated those three options, understood yourself well enough to prioritize the three, and considered your various values and faced the tradeoffs involved. And, based on all that, you acted.

So that's the core of the career decision-making process...or at least what it should be. The unfortunate fact is that even today, most workers still just fall into their careers. Very few people really investigate or actually plan their work, and, in many cases, that's primarily fueled by anxiety. They just try to grab hold of something and don't give the decision-making process enough time.

Whether you're starting out in the workplace or starting over, don't let that happen to you. Beginning with the next chapter, give it enough time.

Career Matchmaking: The "Strong" Evidence

WHEN YOU'RE TRYING TO DECIDE on a career, part of the self-assessment process includes identifying your personal interests. Simply put, given your druthers, what do you like to do? For some people, this is a piece of cake. They can easily elaborate on what they enjoy doing on the job and how they like to spend their leisure time. They may know that they have similar—or different—interests for work and play.

But many other people find it difficult to define their interests, especially in terms of career activities. Young entry-level career seekers often simply haven't had enough experience to know what they really like to do. And career changers may have never before had the luxury of asking themselves, What am I really interested in doing? Family influences, finances, or other pressures may have pushed them into a line of work years ago, and they dutifully punched in every day.

"They got into what they got into and have simply done it ever since," observes Martin E. Jaffe, manager of the InfoPLACE career information center of Cleveland's Cuyahoga County Public Library. "Now they're ready to look at things in a new light, and they're open to 'process,' such as doing an interest inventory."

▼ ▼ ▼ ▼ ▼ ▼ ▼ ▼

About half a million Strong inventories are administered every year.

The instrument most widely used as part of that process is the *Strong Interest Inventory* (*Strong*). It was developed in the 1920s by Stanford University Professor Edward K. Strong Jr., who believed that people with similar interests are often drawn to the same types of work, enjoy being with others who share those interests, and are likely to do well in a work environment that reflects those interests. The *Strong* is periodically revised to reflect the most current realities of the workforce, and the latest revision was introduced in the summer of 1994. (See "Questions and Answers About the New *Strong Interest Inventory*" on page 20 for more on the revision.)

About half a million *Strong* inventories are administered by qualified professionals every year. The majority (about 65%) are done in educational settings. The rest are given in business settings for career development and organization development. The newest growth of the *Strong* is in outplacement, where it helps experienced workers who are losing their jobs because of corporate downsizings and layoffs to assess a possible career change or transition.

Whether or not you do share similar attitudes and preferences with people who are currently working in an occupation is important, because studies have linked such similarities to making decisions about entering an occupation and subsequently doing well in it. However, the operative word here is *interests*—not ability or intelligence—which the *Strong* does not measure. Just because you are interested in a career does not necessarily mean you have the ability—or even the motivation—to pursue it. For example, becoming a neurosurgeon may sound exciting, but are you ready—psychologically, physically, educationally, and financially—for the eight-plus years of training involved?

Some people take the *Strong* to help them explore a range of alternative careers, to suggest new options, or to confirm a choice they already have in mind. It is also used in mid-career evaluation or before a reentry into the workforce. The results can offer insight into your preferences in lifestyle, learning style, work and leisure pursuits, workplace environment, and potential leadership style.

So what does taking the *Strong* actually involve? It is a list of 317 items that measure your interests in broad areas, particular activities, and 109 different occupations. It does this by asking whether you like, dislike, or are indifferent to various choices in the categories of occupations, school subjects, work-related activities, leisure activities, and types of people; which of two activities you prefer; whether you like to work more with people, things, data, or ideas; and whether you think you possess certain characteristics. The questionnaire generally takes about thirty-five to forty minutes to complete.

For example, you would mark whether you "Like," "Dislike," or are "Indifferent" to school subjects such as industrial arts, sociology, statistics, and nature study. Ditto for activities such as making statistical charts, operating machinery, buying merchandise for a store, giving first aid assistance, or discussing the purpose of life. You have the same choices for how you'd feel about day-to-day contact with various types of people, among them musical geniuses, athletic people, military officers, nonconformists, or prominent business leaders.

Your responses are then compared with the interests of a sample of people in general, and your gender in particular, who are satisfied working in a wide variety of occupations. When your inventory results are analyzed, they are reported in three areas:

- *General Occupational Themes (GOTs)*—your similarity to six overall patterns of individual and vocational interests: Realistic, Investigative, Artistic, Social, Enterprising, and Conventional. (See "Taking a Closer Look at the General Occupational Themes" on page 16 for details on these patterns.)

Taking a Closer Look at the General Occupational Themes

Realistic

These workers prefer to deal with things rather than ideas or people. They like hands-on activities that allow them to use physical strength and mechanical abilities. They prefer to solve concrete problems rather than abstract ones. They enjoy working outdoors, often with plants or animals.

SAMPLE OCCUPATIONS

Engineer
Carpenter
Forester
Police officer

SAMPLE POTENTIAL JOB SKILLS

Work with precision
Operate equipment
Assemble materials

Investigative

These workers have a strong scientific orientation. They prefer to analyze and interpret data and enjoy solving abstract problems. They are curious and observant and prefer working with ideas more than with people.

SAMPLE OCCUPATIONS

Biologist
Computer programmer
Mathematician
Geologist

SAMPLE POTENTIAL JOB SKILLS

Make projections
Collect data
Contribute new ideas

Artistic

These workers place a high priority on self-expression and creativity and have a high appreciation of art, music, and language. Sensitive and emotional, they are innovative and prefer to work in flexible, unstructured environments.

SAMPLE OCCUPATIONS

Musician
Advertising executive
Interior decorator
Art teacher

SAMPLE POTENTIAL JOB SKILLS

Design displays
Write creatively
Interpret languages

- *Basic Interest Scales*—your similarity to twenty-five clusters of work activities within the six GOT areas. Examples of clusters include culinary arts, data management, merchandising, computer activities, mechanical activities, or social service.

- *Occupational Scales*—your similarity to the interests of men and women in 109 specific occupations, such as child care provider, athletic trainer, speech pathologist, college professor, lawyer, and accountant.

Taking a Closer Look at the General Occupational Themes (continued)

Social

These workers are concerned with the welfare of others and look for opportunities to help or serve people. They prefer to solve problems through discussion and have a strong sense of responsibility.

SAMPLE OCCUPATIONS

Nurse
Speech therapist
School teacher
Social worker

SAMPLE POTENTIAL JOB SKILLS

Interview clients
Arrange social functions
Counsel people

Enterprising

These workers prefer environments where they can assume leadership. Often skilled in public speaking, they like to persuade others as to the value of an idea or product. They are adventurous and self-confident.

SAMPLE OCCUPATIONS

Marketing executive
Realtor
Travel agent
Elected public offical

SAMPLE POTENTIAL JOB SKILLS

Negotiate contracts
Manage a department
Make presentations

Conventional

These workers prefer to work for others in a structured and ordered environment, and they want to know precisely what's expected of them. They are concerned with detail and accuracy, and often are good with numbers.

SAMPLE OCCUPATIONS

Banker
Math teacher
Medical records technician
Accountant

SAMPLE POTENTIAL JOB SKILLS

Budget expenses
Plan agendas
Manage data

When your *Strong* results are analyzed, the General Occupational Themes (GOTs) to which you have the greatest similarity will comprise your GOT code. It may be a three-letter code, such as SAE (for Social, Artistic, and Enterprising), or it may be a two- or even one-letter code if you have a score of high interest in only one theme and your scores on the other themes are significantly lower. (In much of the career literature, these codes are commonly referred to as RIASEC codes, for the first letter in each theme, or Holland codes, because they are based on psychologist John L. Holland's theory of personality and vocational types.)

It should be stressed that no one theme fits any one person or occupation exactly. Most people have interests that combine several of the themes to some degree.

The theme titles sometimes confuse those taking the inventory. For example, what does it mean if you score high on the Artistic theme, yet have never brandished a paintbrush or otherwise considered yourself creative? On the *Strong*, Artistic also may signify an interest in or an appreciation of creative forms of expression. Similarly, Conventional has no negative connotation; it certainly doesn't mean you're the kind of person who simply follows the herd and never tries anything new!

For career explorers, a major value of the *Strong* is that it can identify occupational interest *patterns*. Once those patterns have been identified, you can begin to look into specific careers. All the Occupational Scales and Basic Interest Scales are coded to the GOTs. So if your results indicate a pattern of interest in occupations grouped within, say, the Realistic theme, that gives you several options to consider. Also, if you score "Similar" or "Very Similar" on an Occupational Scale, such as restaurant manager, it indicates that you not only like the same things the people currently working in this career like, but that you also dislike the same things they dislike. That means you would probably enjoy the day-to-day work in that job.

As one counselor summarized that scenario, "It's not just that you'll like the job tasks, it's that you'll probably like the same leisure activities as these people; you'll probably like the same school subjects as these people. You're simply going to like hanging around with them— you'll probably want to go have a beer with them at the end of the day!"

So let's say you take the *Strong* and your GOT code turns out to be AE—Artistic and Enterprising. The counselor will then show you a list of the careers on the *Strong* that "match" this same code, as well as all the combinations of those letters. For example, you'd first want to look at the list of occupations coded AE. These include advertising executive, broadcaster, and public relations director.

These occupations have pronounced similarities— communications and marketing roles—but also some differences in terms of the work environments and skills used most.

Also look at occupations that have these two letters within their three-letter code, for example, corporate trainer, English teacher, interior decorator, photographer, public administrator, elected public official, flight attendant, florist, and travel agent.

Where do you find these "code-customized" occupations? When you get your *Strong* results, you can review the booklet *Where Do I Go Next?: Using Your Strong Results to Manage Your Career,* which includes a selection of more than 200 occupations listed by career codes. However, the mother lode list is in the *Dictionary of Holland Occupational Codes: A Comprehensive Cross-Index of Holland's RIASEC Codes With 12,000 DOT Occupations.* This book provides not only the RIASEC code of each occupation but also the federal government's *Dictionary of Occupational Titles* (DOT) code.

That means you should next look up the career(s) you're considering in the *Dictionary of Occupational Titles.* Though the DOT has never won any awards for lively writing, it is comprehensive. In addition to a detailed description of the duties involved in every job (20,000 of them, if you want to know all your options), it also groups related occupations together, which makes it another convenient resource for career explorers.

Every major library or library career center has the DOT and is likely to have the *Holland Dictionary* as well.

This all may seem like a great deal of reading and research and process. But it's all meant to provide food for thought as you learn more about your real interests and what kind of career is most likely to make you eager to get up and go to work each day.

And isn't that why you're doing this in the first place?

▼ ▼ ▼ ▼ ▼ ▼ ▼

The Strong helps people

- *Make career choices*
- *Explore college major options*
- *Change careers*
- *Develop careers*
- *Understand out-placement options*

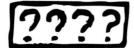

Questions and Answers About the New Strong Interest Inventory

In the following question-and-answer session, researcher and counseling psychologist Allen L. Hammer, who helped develop the 1994 revision of the *Strong*, responds to frequently asked questions about the inventory.

How is the Strong different from other ways of assessing interests?

The *Strong* has been around for over sixty years and has been continually updated, so it has a longer history and more research behind it than all other assessment tools. It has helped more than 30 million people find more interesting and satisfying careers. Studies have shown that it predicts the occupation a person will choose about 65 percent of the time. Strong himself studied a sample where he predicted what occupations people would go into twenty years later, and his predictions proved surprisingly accurate.

How can knowing your interests help in career decisions?

The idea is to increase your self-knowledge so you know how your likes and dislikes can help predict what kinds of jobs will suit you. That can help you choose a career or modify your job so that it fits you better.

Why and how has the Strong been revised?

Our rationale for revising the inventory has always been to add new occupations and to make its occupational database as current as possible. We looked for occupations that represented new opportunities and options in the world of work for students or adults. Then we resampled thirty-six occupations already on the inventory that we thought had changed.

Q&A • Q&A • Q&A • Q&A

When you take the Strong, what types of workers are you being compared to?

The samples are made up of men and women who have been in their particular job for at least three years, who said that they were satisfied with the work, and who were at least twenty-five years of age.

There are currently more than 67,000 men and women in the sample database, almost 40,000 of them new, representing a wide variety of occupations, ethnic groups, and educational levels.

In choosing people for the sample, did you take into account how well they did their jobs?

No. What's important is whether they enjoyed the work and were doing tasks typical of that occupation, based on their job title. For example, a lawyer who said her job title was chief financial officer was not included in the sample for lawyers because that's not typical for the occupation.

Which occupations were added to the revision?

There were fourteen: actuary, audiologist, auto mechanic, bookkeeper, community service organization director, corporate trainer, gardener/groundskeeper, medical records technician, paralegal, small business owner, technical writer, translator, plumber (men only) and child care provider (women only).

Why are there separate male and female samples for the Occupational Scales?

Because men and women still answer the items differently, the scales reflect the differences in people's interests. That's important, because even men and women within the same occupation respond differently to the same items.

One of the goals of the *Strong* is to encourage people to explore a wide range of occupations, including those that may have previously been dominated by one gender.

Q & A • Q & A • Q & A • Q & A

What level of education do the occupations on the inventory require?

The balance is approximately 60 percent professional occupations (those requiring a four-year college degree) and 40 percent vocational/technical occupations that do not require a bachelor's degree.

What information does someone receive after taking the revised Strong?

Your counselor or whomever has administered the inventory should give you a six-page profile of your results. The first page "Snapshot" summarizes your results in the six General Occupational Themes, your top five Basic Interest Scales, and your top ten Occupational Scales, all ranked in order of interest.

The Profile also includes the new Personal Style Scales. These measure your comfort level in four important areas of work and leisure: Leadership Style, Work Style, Learning Environment, and Risk taking/ Adventure. For example, the Work Style scale reflects whether you prefer to work with people or with data, ideas, or things, while the Leadership Style scale indicates whether you like to take charge and direct people, versus leading by doing—in other words, you do a great job and people follow your example. Learning Environment reflects your level of interest in intellectual activities and how comfortable you might be in a traditional academic setting. The Risk Taking/ Adventure scale reflects how comfortable you are about taking risks.

Expanded career reports are available through your counselor, and go into more extensive interpretation of your results, or identify professional occupations related to your code, tied to your management style and preferred work environment.

How the Strong Helped Refine a Career Choice

For Amy Albright, twenty-nine, taking the *Strong* was part of a quest for guidance at an apparent crossroads in her career.

After she had graduated from the University of Wisconsin–Madison in 1989 with a BS in sociology, she took what she calls "a year to regroup" by moving to New Jersey and working in a department store. "I was trying to decide whether to go on to graduate school, but I started to feel that what I needed was a real skill," she explains. She thought that having a "hard" skill, plus her degree, would be especially advantageous in the workplace.

The daughter of a doctor and a nurse, Albright had a long-time exposure to the health field and knew she enjoyed helping people. She decided to go into radiologic technology and moved back to Madison to go to school. She became a certified radiologic (X-ray) technologist in 1993.

She got a job right away, working for a group of orthopedic surgeons. But there was only one other technician at the clinic, and a personality conflict soon developed. The more experienced technician made Albright feel that she wasn't doing a good enough job, and her confidence suffered. However, she was determined to stick it out for a year to make her résumé look better.

When she finally did quit the job in May 1994, Albright says she "never felt so low in my life. I felt I'd made the wrong career choice—and now what was I going to do? I knew that I just had to talk to someone and get some guidance."

Career Profile • Career Profile • Career Profile

Albright went to her alma mater's office of adult career counseling and made an appointment to see a counselor. "The first visit we just talked," explains Albright, "then she gave me the *Strong*." Albright's highest score was in the Social theme, followed by Investigative and Enterprising. (The *Strong* code for female radiologic technologist is RIS—Realistic, Investigative, Social.)

"When we first looked at the *Strong* results, it made me think I shouldn't even be in X-ray," Albright recalls. "But looking closer, when we analyzed everything, it became clear that I am in the right field, just not the best niche. Instead of taking diagnostic X-rays every five minutes of different patients, I need to have a more substantial one-to-one contact with someone. I'd rather be doing an exam that lasts maybe an hour, so I'm kind of getting to know someone and feeling that I am helping that person out. That means getting into MRI (magnetic resonance imaging) or doing CT scans (computer tomography) or ultrasound."

In her current job, Albright is a "floating" technician for five medical clinics, including two urgent care facilities. Since she's been in the job only a few months, she's the "low person on the totem pole," so she hopes to eventually work her way into one of those other areas. She adds, "I also learned from the *Strong* that I work best as part of a team. Right now at some of the clinics I'm the only tech working the shift. For me it's much more fun to talk over cases with the other techs."

Albright knows that it may take awhile to achieve her new goal, but she feels more relaxed just knowing that she's refined what it should be. I didn't feel I'd really given X-ray a fair shot on my first job," she reflects. "The *Strong* results helped me feel that I can follow my instincts, because I didn't make the wrong career choice after all."

My Work, Myself: Personality Type and Your Career

3

HAVE YOU EVER NOTICED that certain kinds of occupations seem to attract certain kinds of people? It's likely that you know a gregarious salesperson, a detail-oriented accountant, or a compassionate counselor. You probably watch one of those peppy sports announcers on your local newscast.

Maybe it's not a coincidence that these workers seem to share certain traits. Maybe each of them knew beforehand which career would best suit their personality and style. If so, then it's likely that they might have discovered their personality type from having taken the *Myers-Briggs Type Indicator*, also known as the MBTI inventory. This assessment tool can give you important insights into your own behavior and help you to better understand and communicate with your colleagues in the workplace.

The MBTI inventory and the *Strong* are commonly used together during the self-assessment process when people are choosing or changing a career. They are valuable because they help you learn more about who you "are," by identifying your interests—through the *Strong*, as discussed in chapter 2—and your personality type, as indicated by the MBTI inventory. Both can also serve to confirm what you already know about yourself. For example, if you prefer to work with a group, if you're energized being around others, then you won't

MBTI Fast Facts

More than two and one-half million people take the MBTI inventory every year. About 70 percent are in business settings; the rest are in the college population. In business, the use and growth of the MBTI inventory is largely related to staff development, management training, and team building. Observers say that's because there's an increasing recognition in productivity-minded companies today that people have to know how to get along with each other and communicate with each other to get things done. The MBTI inventory can help them understand what makes other people tick.

There currently are four versions of the MBTI inventory available. They range from a self-scoring, 94-item form popular in business-related workshops to the most extensive 290-item form often used in one-on-one career counseling. The inventory must be given to you by a counselor or other professional trained in its use and interpretation.

be surprised to learn that you're an Extraverted type on the MBTI inventory or that your code on the *Strong* includes a Social theme. When you are trying to decide on an occupation, it can be very reassuring if you find yourself drawn to one that is known for being popular among people with interests and preferences that are similar to yours.

But let's get more specific about personality type. If you have not encountered this concept before, here's a brief primer—we'll call it Type 101.

Personality assessment by type is based on four factors, as shown in the chart on the following page.

In each pair of preferences, you fall more on one side of the scale or the other. So you are either E or I (for Extraversion or Introversion), S or N (for Sensing or Intuition), T or F (for Thinking or Feeling), and J or P (for Judging or Perceiving). Each combination of letters represents a different kind of personality—for a total of sixteen possible personality types. For example, if the indicator reveals that your preferences are Extraverted, Sensing, Feeling, and Judging, then your personality type is ESFJ. An Introverted, Intuitive, Thinking, Perceiving type is an INTP, and so on.

You do, of course, use *all* the preferences in your daily life; it's just that you have a natural preference for one over another. The MBTI inventory reveals how you prefer to operate, but that doesn't mean that's always how you do operate. These four elements are not the sum total of your personality; it also includes such factors as your values, your character traits, and your intelligence.

So how does any of this figure into choosing or enjoying a career? Your personality type tells you about such basic needs as how you like to take in information and how you like to make decisions—which are, of course, important elements of any job. Knowing your preferred methods of operation can indicate how satisfied you will be in certain types of work and how likely it is that you will enjoy the everyday tasks and responsibilities that will be expected of you.

Your Personality Preferences

1 *How You Prefer to Focus Your Attention or Direct Your Energy*

EXTRAVERSION (the outer world of people and things) or

INTROVERSION (the inner world of concepts and ideas)

This is the E/I preference. Seventy-five percent of people are Extraverted types.

2 *How You Prefer to Process Information*

SENSING (focusing on facts, practical experience) or

INTUITION (focusing on possibilities, making inferences)

This is the S/N preference (N for intuition, because "I" denotes Introversion). Seventy-five percent of people are Sensing types.

3 *How You Prefer to Make Decisions*

THINKING (based on logic) or

FEELING (based on values)

This is the T/F preference. The population is about equally divided between Thinking and Feeling types.

4 *How You Prefer to Live*

JUDGING (in a structured, orderly way) or

PERCEIVING (in a spontaneous, flexible way)

This is the J/P preference. Again, the population is about 50-50 in terms of the number of Judging and Perceiving types.

Personality Types and Workstyle

The thumbnail descriptions in the "Personality Types and How They Work" chart at the end of this chapter can give you an idea of how different personality types prefer to operate in work situations. If you don't already know your type, these examples should start to give you some clues.

A few words about the preference labels: They don't always mean exactly what they may seem to mean. For example, being a Judging type doesn't mean you're rigidly judgmental or that you never go with your gut feelings in making a decision. Being a Perceiving type doesn't mean that you're automatically astute at assessing people or situations, nor does being an Introverted type necessarily mean you're shy and withdrawn. On occasion, you might actually be the life of the party— but then it's likely that you'll need to go home and "recharge your batteries" with some quiet solitude!

There are no right or wrong types. The world—and most certainly the workplace—needs them all. One thing counselors often say they value most about the MBTI inventory is that it is very affirming: It says everybody is okay—just different—and we need to learn to value those differences. Each one of these preferences is a gift, and if you can learn to understand and value *your* gift, you're going to be much happier. That's why MBTI co-creator Isabel Briggs Myers (see "The Roots of Type" on page 29) called her book about personality type *Gifts Differing*.

As explained in *Gifts Differing,* the S or N preference seems to have the most influence on occupational choice. Sensing types are drawn to occupations that let them deal regularly with facts (such as accounting), whereas Intuitives prefer situations in which they can consider all the possibilities (such as research science).

According to Myers, the next most important preference influencing occupation is T or F. People whose preference is Thinking prefer to work with objects, machinery, or theories—all of which can be handled "logically." Conversely, Feeling types prefer handling matters involving people and how they can be persuaded or helped.

Some examples might be helpful: If you're an Extraverted type, you probably need to find a work environment where you can have a lot of interaction with people. If you're Introverted, you will want to know if you'll have opportunity to quietly concentrate on what you need to do. If you're a Judging type, you need to find a work situation that is reasonably predictable and organized, where you can regularly come to closure and feel a sense of accomplishment. If you are a Perceiving type, it will be important to find out if the career you're considering involves making a lot of decisions every day. If it does, you probably won't be happy.

However, it must be stressed that *all* types are found in virtually all jobs. As its title says, the MBTI inventory is an indicator—not a dictator—of what you might do or become.

"If you're going to take the MBTI inventory, be sure you're taking it as who you naturally are—your 'shoes-off self,'" advises Nancy Pool Dixson, director of the Career Center at the University of Denver. "A lot of people take it in a work context, perhaps as part of a team-building project. Sometimes that means they may feel pressured to be a certain role, which may not be natural for them." To get true results, Dixson says, you must answer the way you really feel.

A typical question on the MBTI inventory might be, "Does following a schedule appeal to you, or cramp you?" or "Which word in each pair appeals to you more: Fascinating or sensible? Convincing or touching?"

After you take the MBTI inventory, you will get your four-letter type and often a handout explaining the eight preferences. Your counselor can also present you with a Career Report that tells you which occupations seem to be most attractive to someone with your preferences.

The Roots of Type

 The concept of personality type began with Swiss psychologist Carl Jung, who believed that human behavior could be predicted. In 1921, Jung published his theory of psychological types. A young thinker named Katharine C. Briggs read it and exclaimed something along the lines of, "Eureka! This is exactly what I'm researching, too!" She began a serious study of Jung's work, and eventually her daughter, Isabel Briggs Myers, became her partner.

The pioneering research and writing of this mother-and-daughter team established the sixteen personality types. In the 1940s, they began developing the Myers-Briggs Type Indicator. The MBTI inventory was one of the first personality instruments designed not to measure pathology, but to observe behavior patterns in normal, healthy people in order to help them understand how they might differ in going about living their lives.

Over the decades, the MBTI inventory has been refined and improved and scientifically validated. Today, it is the most widely used and respected personality inventory for the general public.

For further exploration, library career areas generally have the *Atlas of Type Tables*, which tells how often you'll find the sixteen personality types in hundreds of occupations. If you are considering a career change, this information can start you thinking about exploring job possibilities that may not have appealed to you, or even occurred to you before. Let them occur to you—don't make any knee-jerk dismissals at this stage.

But what if your test results don't show an affinity for the career you have in mind? Let's say you're working with a career counselor, and the MBTI inventory reveals that you're an ISTJ—a Sensing type. You tell the counselor that you're thinking about becoming a psychotherapist. When she looks up ISTJ in the MBTI database, she'll see that the occupation of psychotherapist is very far down the list for that type. That's because the great majority of psychotherapists are Intuitive types. The very essence of their job entails looking at possibilities in people and thinking in the abstract—exactly what Sensing types like you generally do not prefer.

Your counselor would then point out that if you want to pursue psychotherapy, you're not going to have much company in terms of people who think the way you do. You're going to have different ways of doing things as a therapist, a different approach. So do you forget it? Not so fast.

When career counselors interpret the MBTI inventory (or the *Strong*), they are trying to help you look at the fit between your personality and the personalities of many people in that occupation, and the kinds of tasks you might be doing. If that fit looks good, terrific. If it doesn't, then it is the counselor's role to make you aware of what problems or obstacles you may have to overcome. Not to talk you out of it, just to make sure you understand all the implications of possibly "going against type."

As Isabel Briggs Myers observed,

> When an occupation is seldom chosen by people of their own type, the prospective workers should investigate the job thoroughly. If they still want to pursue it and are willing to make the effort required to be understood by their co-workers, they may be valued as contributors of abilities that are rare among their co-workers.

In other words, you may rock the boat, but you also may be the one who steers it in a new direction.

But note Myers' emphasis on investigating the job thoroughly. That process includes reading and networking and information interviewing and job shadowing and possibly interning or working as a temporary employee, all of which will be discussed in later pages.

As you go through your career exploration process, you should give careful attention to any occupations that appear on *both* your *Strong* and MBTI profiles. These areas are likely to suit both your personality style and your interest patterns, thus increasing the possibility of a good fit. But there are also several other factors to consider in your decision, and you can begin to define them in the next chapter.

▼ ▼ ▼ ▼ ▼ ▼ ▼ ▼

To find out more about the MBTI, the Strong, or any of the print resources listed below, contact:

Consulting Psychologists Press, Inc.
3803 East Bayshore Road
Palo Alto, CA 94303
800-624-1765

RESOURCES ON PERSONALITY TYPE

- *Atlas of Type Tables* by Gerald P. Macdaid, Mary H. McCaulley, and Richard Kainz, published by Center for Applications of Psychological Type. Includes type tables for hundreds of occupations.

- *Do What You Are* by Paul D. Tieger and Barbara Barron-Tieger, published by Little, Brown and Company. Includes thoughtful discussions about how the different MBTI types function in the workplace, with detailed case studies.

- *Gifts Differing* by Isabel Briggs Myers with Peter B. Myers, published by Davies-Black Publishing.

Personality Types and How They Work

Extraverted Types	Introverted Types
Like variety and action	Like quiet for concentration
Tend to be faster than others, dislike complicated procedures	Tend to be careful with details, dislike sweeping statements
Are often good at greeting people	Have trouble remembering names and faces
Are often impatient with long, slow jobs	Tend not to mind working without interruption on one project for a long time
Are interested in the results of their job	Are interested in the ideas behind their job
Often don't mind the interruption of answering the telephone	Dislike telephone intrusions and interruptions
Often act quickly, sometimes without thinking	Like to think a lot before they act, and sometimes don't act
Like to have people around	Work contentedly alone

Includes descriptions of all sixteen MBTI types, including explanations of the influence each type can have on learning, career choice, and relationships.

- *Introduction to Type in Careers* by Allen L. Hammer, published by Consulting Psychologists Press. Includes interactive exercises that provide information about personality types and career matching.

Personality Types and How They Work *(continued)*

Thinking Types	Feeling Types
Don't readily show emotion; are often uncomfortable dealing with people's feelings	Tend to be very aware of other people and their feelings
May hurt people's feelings without knowing it	Enjoy pleasing people, even in unimportant things
Like analysis and putting things into logical order	Like harmony; office feuds may badly disturb their efficiency
Can operate effectively without harmony	Need occasional praise
Tend to decide impersonally, sometimes without paying attention to people's wishes	Often let decisions be influenced by their own or others' likes and dislikes
Need to be treated fairly	Tend to be sympathetic
Are able to reprimand people or fire them when necessary	Dislike telling people unpleasant things
Are more analytically oriented; respond more easily to people's thoughts	Are more people oriented; respond more easily to people's values

- *Introduction to Type in Organizations* by Sandra Krebs Hirsh and Jean Kummerow, published by Consulting Psychologists Press. This guide describes all sixteen MBTI types and their preferences in the workplace.

Personality Types and How They Work (continued)

Sensing Types	Intuitive Types
Dislike new problems unless there are standard ways to solve them	Like solving new problems
Like an established way of doing things	Dislike doing the same things over and over
Enjoy using skills already learned more than learning new ones	Enjoy learning a new skill more than using it
Work steadily, with a realistic idea of how long it will take	Work in bursts of energy powered by enthusiasm, with slack periods in between
Are patient with routine details	Are impatient with routine details
Are impatient when details get complicated	Are patient with complicated situations
Seldom make errors of fact	May make errors of fact
Tend to be good at precise work	Dislike taking time for precision

Personality Types and How They Work (continued)

Judging Types	Perceiving Types
Work best when they can plan their work and follow their plan	Adapt well to changing situations
Like to get things settled and finished	Like to leave things open for last-minute changes
Reach closure by deciding too quickly	Postpone decisions while searching for options
May not notice new things that need to be done	May postpone unpleasant jobs
Want only the essentials needed to begin a project	Want to know all about a new project
Tend to be satisfied once they reach a decision on a thing, situation, or person	Tend to be curious and welcome new light on a thing, situation, or person

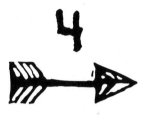

Beyond Interests and Type: How to Complete Your Career Profile

LET'S ASSUME AT THIS POINT that you will take or already have taken the MBTI inventory to learn about your personality style, and the *Strong* to get some direction about your preferred work and leisure activities.

Those are valuable tools, but by themselves they don't provide all the information you want in order to make a thoughtful career decision. As explained in chapter 1, there are several elements involved in a thorough self-assessment. In this chapter, you will get that additional information, particularly in terms of the work values that are important to you and the skills you really want to use in your next job.

The idea here is to start filling in the framework of your occupational big picture, what we'll call your Outline for Success (see page 58). After you complete the various self-assessment exercises in this chapter (take your time on these—nothing is based on beating the clock), you will have a two-page summary of yourself. It will reflect the values and skills you want to employ in your next job, your interests (as defined by your RIASEC code), your personality type (as indicated by the MBTI inventory), and a few other factors that are important specifically for you.

As you progress with your career research, the Outline for Success will provide a quick and visual reminder of what you're trying to achieve—work that satisfies you on as many levels as possible. You can pull information from it to compare and contrast your most promising occupations on the Matchmaker Chart later in this book (see chapter 8). There are also some "food-for-thought" elements here that are fun and may spark some creative thinking.

So get out a pencil and a few sheets of paper, kick off your shoes, and get settled in your favorite chair.

Defining Your Work Values

Perhaps you've never really thought about it before, but we all have values that we attach to the work we do. Values are why someone becomes a public servant, strives to be president of the corporation, or Employee of the Year. They need to give and get something from their occupation that goes beyond simply earning a salary.

Values relate to your decisions about how you will live. The kinds of things and people you choose to include in your daily life are determined in part by your values. When it comes to making a career choice, considering what's important to you increases the likelihood that you'll make a satisfactory decision. But you need to move beyond having an intuitive sense of those values; you need labels so that you can identify them and thus determine if they can be met.

The following exercise can help you do that. But as you complete it, be honest with yourself. If money, power, recognition, and status are important to you at work, then don't try to convince yourself that they're really not. Conversely, if you place a high value on "doing good" and serving others, you must decide if that need outweighs choosing a career that's more lucrative but less fulfilling.

What Are Your Work Values?

 **Directions:** *As you read the list of values, circle the appropriate letter to indicate if the work value is very important (V), moderately important (M), or not important (N) to you.*

High Income
Finding a job that will allow me to make a lot of money   V   M   N

Prestige
Having a job that will give me visibility or status in my
community   V   M   N

Professional Recognition
Earning the respect of colleagues in my field   V   M   N

Helpfulness
Doing work that directly helps people in need or serves
a cause   V   M   N

Fast Pace
Having work that requires me to be thinking or doing
almost all the time   V   M   N

Autonomy
Being able to work independently and make choices
about priorities and organization   V   M   N

Leadership
Using my ability to motivate and direct others in a
supervisory capacity   V   M   N

Time Flexibility
Being able to set my own hours and arrange my day as I
think best   V   M   N

Continue ⟶

Intellectual Challenge
Having work that stimulates my mind and requires me to
stretch intellectually   V   M   N

Physical Challenge
Having work that involves physical effort to get the job
done   V   M   N

Sense of Mission
Using my job to make the world a better place to live   V   M   N

Creativity
Having the opportunity to express myself through
my work   V   M   N

Team Member
Working in a group toward a common goal   V   M   N

Personal Recognition
Working for a boss and/or organization that notices and
rewards my efforts   V   M   N

Contact With Others
Having a lot of face-to-face interaction with the public
or co-workers   V   M   N

Sociability
Being able to enjoy camaraderie with others at work who
share my interests   V   M   N

Competition
Engaging in activities in which I must do my best and
which result in my being on a winning or losing side   V   M   N

Pressure
Working under the stimulation of deadlines   V   M   N

Continue ⟶

Diversity and Change
Participating in work activities that are often different day
to day   V   M   N

Security
Being able to have a reasonable expectation that my job or
skills will remain in demand   V   M   N

Problem Solving
Finding solutions to significant problems as the main focus
of my work   V   M   N

Influence
Having work that allows me to have a direct impact on
people's lives   V   M   N

Excitement/Adventure
Having responsibilities that often involve risk taking
and/or a degree of excitement   V   M   N

Predictability
Having a job with day-to-day responsibilities that hold few
surprises   V   M   N

Power
Knowing I'm "in charge" and that people look to me for
direction and authority   V   M   N

Now, go through your choices in the exercise and
find the values you identified as very important. Even
if there are a dozen, try your best to define which ones
comprise your top five values. Once you've narrowed
it down to the top five, then write them in the Work
Values area of your Outline for Success (see page 58).

What Skills Do You Want to Use?

Just because you do something well doesn't automatically mean that you like doing it. You may be a whiz at totaling up a dinner check, but that doesn't necessarily mean you'd adore a career in accounting. In other words, a competence is not always a preference. The ideal is to have an ability, matched by your interest in using it.

"There's a difference between what I would call gifts and what I would call aptitudes or skills," observes Ilene Rudman, a career counselor with Radcliffe Career Services in Cambridge, Massachusetts, and a psychotherapist in private practice. "Gifts are the things we do for the pure pleasure of it, things that we don't even think of as skills because they're just what we do naturally. Those are the things I'm really interested in helping people begin to identify. For instance, I'm a good conference planner, though I don't do it with love. But I'm a really good listener, and I like to think I do that with a lot of love." Indeed, Rudman changed her own career so she could listen to people. After twenty years of designing employment and training programs for governmental agencies, including the U.S. Department of Labor, she ultimately grew tired of "designing programs for people I never saw," and five years ago she segued into career counseling.

Have you ever really thought about where *your* basic affinity lies?

FUNCTIONAL SKILLS: YOU CAN TAKE THEM WITH YOU

As explained in chapter 1, functional skills literally are the "workhorses" of your skills portfolio—the competencies that you can take with you as you move from job to job.

The U.S. Department of Labor segments the world of work into three basic areas: data, people, or things. The divisions are fairly self-defining. If you prefer working with *data,* you enjoy responsibilities such as doing research, developing theories, analyzing quantitative material, or "crunching numbers." If you enjoy helping or serving *people,* you would enjoy activities such as coaching, leading, persuading, or educating others. If you prefer working with *things,* you probably like repairing or operating machinery, construction projects, or otherwise working with your hands.

Many career development professionals have suggested that the Labor Department add a fourth category: ideas. (The computerized career guidance program, DISCOVER, is based on these four categories.) Would you like to have an impact on data, people, or things by using your ideas to devise new processes and systems, solve social problems, or create industrial designs? If so, then you probably prefer working with *ideas.*

The following table gives you a brief sample of how various skills fall into these four categories.

What Are Your Transferable Skills?

DATA SKILLS	PEOPLE SKILLS	THINGS SKILLS	IDEAS SKILLS
Analyzing	Managing	Repairing	Editing
Researching	Supervising	Wiring	Writing
Computing	Counseling	Distributing	Drawing
Designing	Advising	Handling	Composing
Forecasting	Negotiating	Loading	Designing
Reporting	Training	Assembling	Researching

Reproduced with permission of InfoPLACE Counseling Staff, Cuyahoga County Public Library System, 1994.

At the InfoPLACE career information center of the Cuyahoga County Public Library in Maple Heights, Ohio, participants in career decision workshops are asked to arrange by preference the work activities in the exercise shown on the following page.

Which Transferable Skills Do You Want to Use?

Directions: Go through the checklist and mark off the skills that interest you the most, the ones you want to use on a regular basis in your occupation.

❑ Researching/investigating data (Data)

❑ Teaching/training/instructing people (People)

❑ Visualizing ideas (Ideas)

❑ Renovating things (Things)

❑ Synthesizing and creating new ideas (Ideas)

❑ Collecting information (Data)

❑ Curing/treating/rehabilitating people (People)

❑ Computing and calculating data (Data)

❑ Managing/supervising/leading/ motivating/selling (People)

❑ Operating/flying/driving things (Things)

❑ Writing ideas (Ideas)

❑ Entertaining/hosting/greeting people (People)

❑ Proofreading/editing data (Data)

❑ Designing art, literature, music, new concepts (Ideas)

❑ Keyboarding/typing/inputting data (Data)

❑ Advocating/lobbying on behalf of people (People)

❑ Repairing/servicing/setting up things (Things)

❑ Evaluating ideas (Ideas)

❑ Maintaining and cleaning things (Things)

❑ Finding solutions to problems (Ideas)

❑ Programming and documenting data (Data)

❑ Regulating, controlling, and monitoring things (Things)

❑ Counseling/advising people (People)

❑ Building and constructing things (Things)

Now, look at the skills you checked off in the exercise. Do the skills you prefer fall into any one category? Each item on the list could, of course, be further defined into hundreds of specific job tasks. But what you are looking for here is an overall pattern.

Now, of all the skills you marked, choose the top five that you would prefer to use in a new career or new job. Then take a sheet of paper and write a short, specific example of how you've used that skill before with an "I" statement. For example, someone who marked "managing and supervising people" might write, "I supervised forty production employees for two years and felt I did a good job of motivating them." Or someone who gave a high ranking to "computing and calculating data" might recall, "I computed the total labor costs for a $10 million construction project." Remind yourself what you've accomplished already. Don't overlook volunteer projects or other situations that weren't officially "work."

Now, are those five skills the ones you want to offer your next employer? Rank them in order from 1 to 5. Now write them down on the Functional Skills area of your Outline for Success on page 58.

ADAPTIVE SKILLS: YOUR PERSONAL QUALITIES AND CAREER CHOICE

Adaptive skills are also called *self-management skills* or personal traits and characteristics. They are the behavioral qualities that we learn as we grow up in the world. We use them to fit (or adapt) ourselves in to a variety of environments, starting with home, school, friends, and, finally, the world of work. Along with your functional skills, your adaptive skills today are critical to your success on the job: Poor adaptive skills is the reason most frequently cited by employers for job firings.

Many personality traits can be qualified as skills or aptitudes because they allow you to *accomplish* things. On the job, the expression of these characteristics plays a big role in your effectiveness, your perfor- mance, and your ultimate satisfaction in the work. For example, if it's important to you to have work in which you can be creative and innovative, you are

~~~~~~

How Do Your Skills, Interests, and Type Match Up?

Certain skill sets coincide with MBTI type preferences and RIASEC code vocational interests, as this table shows. For the interest areas or preferences in parentheses, the skill set is important but less so than with the preceding groups.

SKILL SETS	RIASEC CODE	MBTI PREFERENCES
Data	Conventional	Sensing
People	Social, Enterprising	Extraverted, Feeling
Things	Realistic, (Conventional)	Sensing, Judgmental
Ideas	Investigative, Artistic	Intuitive, Thinking, (Feeling)

~~~~~~

Reproduced with permission of InfoPLACE Counseling Staff.

bound to be unhappy in a job where everything is done "by the book" and reviewed by committee. The recognition of your positive personal qualities and characteristics is also vitally important in building your self-esteem, which in turn helps you to forge ahead and act on your career goals.

The exercise on page 48 contains an extensive list of adaptive skills. The list has purposely been developed with some redundancy or overlap; there are different ways of saying and perceiving things that may be easier to recognize as one of your adaptive skills. It's all right for there to be some duplication in the items you check off.

As you go through the list, check the qualities that you prefer to have in your worklife. As you read each adaptive skill, preface it in terms of "I am...detail oriented" (or "I have...good insight") or "I would like to be" (or "to have"). If there are other qualities important to you that are not listed here, go ahead and include them in the area marked "Others."

From your check marks in the exercise, select up to five adaptive skills that you would most like to use in your worklife, which you *also* consider to be at an acceptable level of development. If several skills appear the same or similar, group them together on one line to form a cluster of related qualities.

Then, rank your top five qualities: 1 for the skill you consider to be your strongest, and so on. Then transfer these five qualities to the Adaptive Skills area on your Outline for Success on page 59.

As you go through the career selection process, you might want to check your skills lists from time to time to see if any of your preferences have changed, especially if you enjoy doing many things. This is also true for your work values. However, it is likely that the ones you deem most essential will always be among the top two or three.

Brainstorm!

As you are gathering information about yourself—what you can do, enjoy doing, and care about doing—it's also helpful to take time out to brainstorm about where those interests might lead. Here are several ways InfoPLACE asks workshop participants to brainstorm career options. Don't judge the idea yet, just write it down. Try to generate as many appealing job titles as you can. The responses don't have an official spot on your Outline for Success, they're just intended to help get you thinking "outside the lines."

1. Reflect on your childhood dreams and fantasies. What did you always want to be when you grew up?

2. Scan the work classified ads in the Sunday edition of your major newspaper. Circle any ad that attracts you. Don't worry about your qualifications at this point.

Ask Yourself One Important Question

There is one question that might summarize self-assessment. Career columnist, author, and consultant Marilyn Moats Kennedy of Wilmette, Illinois, suggests you ask yourself this: Of all the things I've ever done in my life, what has given me the most pleasure? Don't discount the possibility of working at something you love.

"I had a client who was laid off by a major retailer after seventeen years of buying men's furnishings," Kennedy explains. "He got another job as a sales rep, but was soon laid off again. One day I asked him this question and he said, 'The only thing that has given me sustained pleasure is golf.'

"At age seventeen he'd known that golf was the passion of his life, but he'd taken a 'sensible' job. Finally, at forty-four, he decided it was time to do what he wanted. He's giving lessons at a public golf course, and soon he'll qualify to become a pro."

Kennedy adds, "Career planning gives a second chance to people who were discouraged from doing what they really wanted to do the first time. Today this man stops in whenever he's nearby just to tell me how happy he is."

How Developed Are Your Adaptive Skills?

Directions: *For only those skills that you want to use in your worklife, check the appropriate box to indicate if the skill is one you would like to use and is adequately developed (AD) or is one you would like to use but needs development (ND).*

PERSONAL QUALITY	AD	ND	PERSONAL QUALITY	AD	ND
Able to get to the heart of problems		☑	Courageous	☐	☑
Able to follow through		☑	Creative	☑	☐
Able to express ideas freely	☑	☐	Credible	☑	☐
Able to get along well with others	☑	☐	Decisive	☐	☑
Able to plan effectively	☐	☑	Dependable	☑	☐
Able to set priorities well	☐	☑	Determined	☐	☐
Able to take criticism	☐	☑	Diplomatic	☑	☐
Able to think things out before acting	☐	☑	Direct	☐	☑
Able to think quickly on my feet	☑	☐	Easygoing	☑	☐
Achievement oriented	☐	☑	Efficient	☐	☑
Adaptable to change	☐	☑	Encouraging of others	☑	☐
Adventurous	☐	☑	Enterprising	☐	☑
Ambitious	☐	☑	Enthusiastic	☐	☑
Analytical	☑	☐	Entrepreneurial	☐	☑
Assertive	☐	☑	Excited about challenge	☐	☑
Attentive to details	☐	☑	Expressive	☐	☑
Bold	☐	☑	Firm	☐	☑
Calm	☑	☐	Flexible	☐	☑
Challenge seeking	☐	☑	Farsighted	☐	☑
Committed to personal growth	☐	☑	Genuine	☑	☐
Communicative	☐	☑	Goal oriented	☐	☑
Competent	☐	☑	Good judgment	☐	☐
Competitive	☐	☑	Good listener	☑	☐
Concentration	☐	☑	Good sense of self	☐	☑
Conscientious	☑	☐	Good team player	☑	☐
Considerate	☑	☐	Gregarious	☐	☑
Cool under fire	☐	☑	Hardworking	☑	☐
Cooperative	☑	☐	Helpful	☑	☐
Cost conscious	☐	☑	Honest	☑	☐
			Humanistic	☑	☐
			Idealistic	☑	☐
			Imaginative	☑	☐
			Independent	☐	☑
			Industrious	☐	☐

 Continue ⟶

PERSONAL QUALITY	AD	ND	PERSONAL QUALITY	AD	ND
Informal	☑	☐	Realistic	☑	☐
Initiative	☐	☑	Relaxed	☐	☐
Innovative	☐	☑	Resourceful	☐	☑
Integrity	☑	☐	Responsible	☑	☐
Intellectual	☐	☑	Risk taker	☐	☐
Intelligent	☑	☐	Secure	☐	☑
Intuitive	☑	☐	Self-confident	☐	☑
Levelheaded	☑	☐	Self-directed	☐	☑
Likable	☑	☐	Self-expressive	☐	☑
Logical	☐	☑	Self-improvement oriented	☐	☐
Methodical	☐	☑	Self-starting	☐	☑
Moral	☑	☐	Self-sufficient	☑	☐
Motivated	☐	☑	Sense of humor	☐	☑
Motivating	☐	☑	Service oriented	☑	☐
Natural	☐	☑	Sincere	☑	☐
Objective	☑	☐	Socially adept	☑	☐
Optimistic	☐	☑	Sophisticated	☐	☑
Organized	☐	☑	Spontaneous	☐	☑
Original	☐	☑	Straightforward	☑	☐
Outgoing	☐	☑	Strong sense of conviction	☑	☐
Patient	☐	☑	Systematic	☐	☑
People oriented	☐	☑	Tactful	☑	☐
Perceptive	☑	☐	Team player	☑	☐
Persistent	☑	☐	Thorough	☐	☑
Persuasive	☐	☑	Trustworthy	☑	☐
Poised	☐	☑	Unpretentious	☑	☐
Politically aware	☑	☐	Venturesome	☐	☑
Positive	☐	☑	Versatile	☐	☑
Practical	☑	☐	Willing to learn	☑	☐
Proactive	☐	☑	Willing to seek and		
Problem solver	☐	☑	take responsibility	☑	☐
Productive	☑	☐	Willing to work steadily		
Professional	☑	☐	for distant goals	☐	☑
Progressive	☐	☑	Witty	☐	☑
Purposeful	☑	☐	Others: _____	☐	☐
Quick to take initiative	☐	☑	_____	☐	☐

Adapted from *If You Knew Who You Were, You Could Be Who You Are!*
by Gerald M. Sturman, Ph.D. Copyright 1992 by Bierman House,
Bedford, NY. Reprinted with permission.

What If That Lottery Ticket Were a Winner?

 To get your creative juices flowing, many career counselors ask you a version of the following fun and enlightening exercise:

If you won the lottery, what would you do with the money?

What kinds of activities would make you happy? What plans would you make? Would you quit your job tomorrow? After all, most of us work because we must. But what if that financial burden were lifted?

Free your imagination. Just think in terms of your wants. What would you do? Play tennis all day? Read every suspense novel ever published? Open a soup kitchen? An art gallery? Buy a farm and provide a home for unwanted pets? Take a one-year trip around the world? Endow a scholarship program in the arts?

This kind of exercise tends to reveal a blend of your work values and your life values, such as personal growth, helping others, or the desire for excitement and challenge.

As you go through your career decision-making process, come back to this exercise again. Some interests and activities might not even surface the first time you make a conscious effort.

3. Think about all the jobs performed by family, friends, relatives, neighbors—even people written about in newspaper articles or the characters on TV shows. Which ones appeal to you?

4. Pretend you are helping a friend. Review the information you gathered about yourself. If this were your friend's data, what would you suggest that she or he do?

5. What do other people regularly compliment you about or tell you that you do well? If you can't think offhand, call up ten friends and ask them to tell you now.

6. If you haven't done so already, review the *Dictionary of Holland Occupational Codes.* Which job titles that match your RIASEC code appeal to you?

7. If you haven't done so already, review careers in the *Atlas of Type Tables.* Which careers tend to attract people with your MBTI type *and* appeal to you?

"I always like to ask clients what they loved to do when they were children," notes Carol Ellin, a career and job search counselor at Goucher College in Baltimore, Maryland. "What came naturally to them? Career seekers should try to use that. Some people think jobs should be detached from what they've done all along, and they go out and look for something else. But sometimes you don't have to look for it. It's right there."

Identifying Your Life Values

As you tried to "spend" all that lottery money (see sidebar on this page), some of your choices were likely influenced, consciously or otherwise, by your life values.

Many career counselors say that career planning cannot be separated from life planning, which is especially true for experienced workers contemplating a change, as they often have family considerations to weigh. To touch base with some of those often nebulous or hard-to-define elements that guide how you live your life, check off all the values that resonate with you in the exercise on the following page.

Some of the items on the life values list may echo the ones listed on the work values list. Did you find yourself marking similar ones here, too? This can suggest how strongly you feel about the values and the importance of trying to have them satisfied in your next occupation.

Of the life values you checked off, choose the five that are most meaningful to you, and add them to the Life Values area on page 59 of the Outline for Success.

In making a career choice, people sometimes ask counselors whether they should give more weight to their preferences in skills or interests or values. As you might expect, there is no one right answer. "It's different for each person," says Ilene Rudman of Radcliffe Career Services. "And though it doesn't always correlate to age, it often does. When I'm working with younger clients, skills often are more important. They really want to be good at something they enjoy and develop a sense of competence. But as you mature, your values become more critical and you cannot shut them out anymore. Your interests, the things that you have passion for, ask to be recognized."

Rudman adds, "It's a theory I haven't proved yet, and there are exceptions. For example, many young college seniors at Radcliffe are incredibly wise beyond their years, and they have a very strong set of work values that come from having volunteered for much of the time that they've been here. So they come in to the counseling center already knowing what those values are, and there's no way that they're going to give them up. For instance, for some students, having a balance between work and family life is very important, and they might say, 'I'm not willing to give up my life in terms of the hours I put into a job.' Then

What Are Your Life Values?

Directions: Check off all the values below that resonate with you.

☑ *Accomplishment* (achievement, aspiration for excellence)

☑ *Aesthetics* (appreciation of beauty, art, music)

☑ *Affection* (satisfying love relationships, caring, becoming close and intimate with another person)

☑ *Appearance* (physical attractiveness, sex appeal)

❏ *Autonomy* (independence, self-direction, freedom, the right to do what I want)

☑ *Career* (satisfying and successful)

☑ *Creativity* (using imagination, being innovative, problem-solving abilities)

❏ *Devotion* (strong spiritual belief, religious faith)

☑ *Economic security* (comfortable life, freedom from financial worry)

☑ *Education* (intellectual achievement for self, family, or others)

☑ *Emotional well-being* (peace of mind, contentment, freedom from inner conflicts)

☑ *Excitement* (adventure, new experiences, challenges, exploring, being enthusiastic)

☑ *Family well-being* (taking care of loved ones, good family relationships)

☑ *Friendship* (having close friendships, companionship)

☑ *Health* (physical well-being)

☑ *Helping others* (humanitarian desires, serving and working with others)

❏ *Home* (home as an anchor, having a lovely home in a beautiful setting)

❏ *Leadership* (influence, power, control over others, being persuasive)

☑ *Personal growth* (development, use of potential, self-realization)

☑ *Play* (pleasure, fun, leisurely life, travel, sport)

❏ *Prestige* (visible success, recognition, status)

☑ *Responsibility* (accountability, reliability, dependability)

☑ *Stability* (order, predictability, tranquility)

❏ *Other* _____

there are others for whom economic security is enormously important. They're going to value that because they have big loans to pay and their families may not be in a position to help."

More Options: Computer-Aided Self-Assessment

The career or job information centers at many larger libraries may offer patrons the use of computerized career guidance programs. Usually you are asked to book an appointment to use the program, and you may be given anywhere from forty-five minutes to two hours' time on it per visit. Librarians generally report that these programs are fully booked every day.

In general, the programs are very interactive, allowing you to "talk back" to the computer, which then generates career options based on how you reply to various self-assessment questions. If you change your answers, you get different lists of career options. You can also work at your own speed.

As current college students often can find these services on campus, library users tend to be adults who may have been laid off or are looking for a career change. Two of the programs often found in public libraries are DISCOVER and SIGI Plus. Another, Career Design, can be purchased for home use.

DISCOVER

This career planning system is from American College Testing. Libraries are more likely to have the version for colleges and adults, which includes many activities for career changers to help them rate their values and inventory their experiences. DISCOVER can be used in two different ways: the "information only" approach, in which you can go directly to reports about colleges or occupations, or the total "guidance-plus-information" approach, which we'll discuss here.

In "guidance plus," you can go through a step-by-step process of career decision making by answering questions about your interests, abilities, values, and work-related experiences. When you have completed it, you'll be given a list of suggested occupations based on your personal profile, which can include your scores from the MBTI inventory and the *Strong,* if you choose to type them in. Libraries can and usually do add local job market and occupational information to the program. Because the guidance plus process is not completed in one sitting, DISCOVER "remembers" individual clients by creating personal records of their usage, so they can pick up each time where they left off. The entire system is menu driven, with easy-to-follow on-screen instructions.

DISCOVER also arranges related occupations into twenty-four job families of its own categorization. For example, the job family of natural sciences and mathematics includes the following: agricultural scientist, animal scientist, astronomer, biochemist, botanist, chemist, ecologist, geneticist, geographer, geologist, geophysicist, horticulturist, marine biologist, mathematician, meteorologist, oceanographer, operations research analyst, pathologist, pharmacologist, physicist, physiologist, range manager, soil conservationist, statistician, and zoologist. Reviewing such job families can be helpful for sparking ideas about occupations that might not necessarily have occurred to you otherwise but which may fit the information about yourself that you "told" the program.

SIGI PLUS

From the Educational Testing Service, the System of Interactive Guidance and Information (SIGI) Plus Program is divided into eight core sections, each related to a stage in the career decision-making process. Users can switch among sections or bypass them rather than being required to follow a sequential approach. SIGI Plus, which is geared to adults, puts an emphasis on skills because adults generally have a better notion of their skills than do college students.

The program also uses a process they call *layering*, which lets users choose the depth of detail they want in each section. SIGI Plus provides information about hundreds of professions, including salaries and employment opportunities, training or education requirements, and school options. In the "Deciding" section, users can evaluate up to three career choices at a time, including the work they're currently doing.

CAREER DESIGN

Though it is not usually found in libraries, this is another highly regarded career guidance system. It is an extension of the seminar program at the New York-based career consulting firm, Crystal-Barkley Corporation. (The late John C. Crystal was the source of much of the work/life planning philosophy contained in *What Color Is Your Parachute* by Richard N. Bolles.)

Career Design is divided into three areas: "Who am I?," "What do I want?," and "How do I get there?" Through a series of self-discovery exercises, you find some answers and make a plan to act on them. The new Version 2 also includes automated résumé formatting and a personal finances module, which can tell career changers how much they need to earn to sustain their current lifestyle. As it is designed for home use, there is a telephone help line if you have questions. Running the program requires an IBM® or compatible personal computer with 525K available RAM, DOS 2.0 or higher, and 3.85 megabytes of hard disk space. The program's suggested retail price is $99 but can often be obtained at a discount in software stores. For further information and ordering, Career Design Software in Atlanta can be contacted at 800-346-8007.

It can take a workweek of time—perhaps forty hours or more—to finish this thorough program, but that is time well spent if you can define your next career. Besides, attending a Crystal-Barkley seminar costs a few thousand dollars, so this do-it-at-home version is indeed a bargain.

Do You Have Career Compatibility?

If you are currently employed but considering a change, ask yourself the following questions from FEGS, the Federation Employment and Guidance Service. The answers should help you better define the sources of your dissatisfaction before you jump ship. If you are considering a job offer, the same questions can also help you evaluate whether there would be a good "fit" between you and that job.

Are you in the right career?

If you can say that you have interests that are compatible with that field—and, of course, if you have a reasonable amount of ability to back it up—then at least you know there's some fit. The *Strong* is one measure of your interests. You also have to go talk to people to find out what tasks and activities they do in this field and whether those are of interest to you. (These "information interviews" are discussed in detail in chapter 7.)

Are you in the right job?

You can be in the right career but the wrong job. This can be further defined as to whether you're in the right function or role. For example, let's say you're a human resources manager with a large corporation and you're thinking about starting an outplacement consulting firm. That brings in the entrepreneurial role, which requires that you actively market your firm's services. You might be an excellent outplacement counselor but an ineffective marketer, so that would be a poor fit with that job function.

Q & A • Q & A • Q & A • Q & A

Is your style compatible with the people you work with, especially your boss?

This is referred to as *interpersonal compatibility*. It deals primarily with your style versus the style of your supervisor, but it also includes how you interact with your peers, your subordinates, and whether you're in sync with the people around you. The boss, of course, is the crucial player here because she or he has the most effect on your career development.

If you're not in sync with the boss, you must consider your options. You can renegotiate your role with the manager; this takes a lot of assertiveness. You can try to transfer to another position—perhaps you can redesign your job, come up with another title and switch departments—and, with any luck, report to somebody else. Or you might have to leave.

When you are making a decision about taking a job, it's critical to find out who you'd report to and ask questions during the interview about that person's work and management style.

Are you in harmony with the corporate culture or organizational climate?

You could be in the right career and the right job, and even have the "right" manager, but be working in the wrong environment. Every organization has a corporate culture; being in sales at IBM Corporation is not the same as being in sales at Apple Computer. And one social services agency may have a completely different management style than another nonprofit.

So you have to look at the organizational climate in terms of the *company's* values, as executed by the people who run it. You have to try to assess the degree of pressure in the workplace, the kind of stress, how much autonomy you would have. There aren't a lot of books with this information, but you may be able to get some of this from informational interviews or from a former employee.

Outline for Success

Directions: *As you complete the earlier self-assessment exercises, collect the information you gather about yourself and your career goals on this worksheet—it will provide a two-page visual summary of who you are. You can transfer the important criteria from this Summary to the Matchmaker Chart on page 137 as you explore and compare various careers.*

Personality Style—Your MBTI Type _____

Preferred Interest Areas—Your RIASEC Code_____

Self-Assessment Factors

WORK VALUES

Work Value #1 _____

Work Value #2 _____

Work Value #3 _____

Work Value #4 _____

Work Value #5 _____

FUNCTIONAL SKILLS

Functional Skill #1 _____

Functional Skill #2 _____

Functional Skill #3 _____

Functional Skill #4 _____

Functional Skill #5 _____

Continue ⟶

ADAPTIVE SKILLS

Adaptive Skill #1 _____

Adaptive Skill #2 _____

Adaptive Skill #3 _____

Adaptive Skill #4 _____

Adaptive Skill #5 _____

LIFE VALUES

Life Value #1 _____

Life Value #2 _____

Life Value #3 _____

Life Value #4 _____

Life Value #5 _____

OTHER CONSIDERATIONS

Minimum salary requirements:_____

Traveling limitations?_____

Possibility of telecommuting?_____

Possibility of relocating?_____

Reproduced with permission of InfoPLACE Counseling Staff.

Getting Out Your Library Card: Starting Your Research

THINGS REALLY ARE STARTING to get interesting now, don't you think? You know (or will know) your personality type and have made a list of the various occupations that suit people with characteristics like yours. You have (or will have) a RIASEC code of your interests, and the list of careers that attract the people who share those interests. You're becoming aware of the values that matter to you in the workplace and the kinds of skills you'd prefer to use on your next job.

So you already have some careers in mind, or you may be browsing a general job family, looking for the most kindred occupation. But can you say yet that you really know what any of these workers actually *do* all day? Do you know what kinds of skills and experiences and personal qualities they need to perform their jobs well? Do you know what salaries they earn and what their work environments are like? Do you know whether the employment picture in their fields is encouraging or not? Are you aware of the biggest problems facing the industries on your list? Or the latest developments that are altering job descriptions and the skills employees need to succeed in that field?

If you don't, there's terrific news: Plenty of people do know—and they've already made it their life's work to explain it all for you in books and periodicals and on videocassettes. And it's all waiting for your purview at the public library.

But, you say, you haven't set foot in a library since you handed in that last college term paper twelve years ago! Well, fasten your seatbelt: you're in for an exciting—and informative—ride.

You'll find that today's librarians still are pleased to recommend a good book, but these "infosurfers" can also introduce you to new technology and offer valuable service during every step of your career research. They can sit you down at a computer terminal to research companies, recommend career videos, suggest you try a career planning software program, and sign you up for a résumé-writing workshop in the library's career center. All before lunch.

It could be said that libraries "ain't just books" anymore. A 1992 survey by the American Library Association (ALA) revealed that almost 80 percent of public libraries that serve areas of 100,000 people or more offer their patrons CD-ROM products or remote database searching (more on that later). Also, more than 60 percent provide personal computers (PCs) and software for the public to use. For example, you might use the library's copy of WordPerfect or résumé-writing software to update your career history.

Libraries, of course, have always been in the business of connecting people with information—it's just that today an increasing number of them are doing it on the cutting edge. One example: As of August 1994, the North Suburban Library System in Illinois was to have forty-six personal computers hooked up for direct public access to that behemoth of online information, the Internet (see chapter 6). So those folks who don't have a computer at home—and most Americans still don't—will be able to explore the limitless resources of the much-talked-about information superhighway for free. And many other libraries around the country are starting to do the same.

"Libraries are not the on-ramps to the information superhighway—they *are* the information superhighway," asserts George M. Needham, executive director of the Public Library Association, a division of the ALA. "Yet the public has a badly outmoded idea of what libraries are, and almost no idea of what they can be."

In other words, get thee to your local branch and find out what's been happening in your absence.

The first highly technological breakthrough you're likely to discover is that there are no more paper cuts. Hundreds of libraries have replaced those drawers upon drawers of index card catalogs with PAC terminals —Public Access Catalogs. You may not even have to leave your living room; many libraries offer people with home or office computers the option of dialing directly into library computer files.

So to check the PAC holdings at that particular library—or its entire system—you type in the subject, book title, or author you're looking for, and the results will show up on the screen. A PAC is often connected to a printer, so you can make a hard copy printout of your resource list and then hit the book shelves to find them.

For a career researcher, the reference librarians in a job information center—often found at a large library or regional center—are so valuable that they may deserve to be remembered in your will. They can save you time and energy and not a small amount of frustration. This is not to say you make a sport of "stump the librarian" with a bizarre request or expect one to do all your research for you, but it's amazing how many people will spend hours stumbling around unfamiliar bookstacks or being mystified by computerized catalogs without asking for help from the person sitting at the desk marked "Information." Also, many libraries have put together bibliographies on their specific career selections and may have a handout showing which titles they have and where they can be found (see "First-Timer Tip: Research by the Numbers" on page 64).

> ## *Drive Onto the Information Superhighway*
>
> The American Library Association reports that nearly 80 percent of public libraries in areas with 100,000 or more people offer their patrons CD-ROM products or online database searches.

First-Timer Tip: Research by the Numbers

If you're not exactly sure what book (or career!) you're looking for and you just want to browse the shelves, it can be helpful to know that libraries that use the Dewey decimal classification system of call numbers often group their career books in three particular numbered areas. ("Nearby" numbers will be similar.)

331.70—include the "information about information" vocational guidance and training resources, such as indexes, directories, guides, and sourcebooks. Books such as *The Enhanced Guide for Occupational Exploration* or *Vocational Careers Sourcebook* are in this category.

371.42—include many of the career books and series that give general industry overviews as well as individual books on specific occupations. For example, the VGM Career Horizons series of more than 100 titles (e.g., *Opportunities in Real Estate, Opportunities in Robotics Careers*) are found here.

650.14—include many of the hands-on and how-to career books: how to write a résumé, how to write a business plan, how to plan or change careers, how to deal with losing a job, how to look for a job, and so on. A very productive area in which to browse.

If you need materials not found at your library, the staff can request an interlibrary loan to get them for you. This can involve scouring the rest of your city or county's system, college libraries, special libraries, and state or even national sources. For example, many libraries that don't carry the periodical you need will contact the location that does have it. It may be photocopied for you and sent to your local library for you to pick up, or they might even be able to fax it to you. Often this service is free.

Also, virtually every library career center has additional resources specific to that state and/or city—usually a directory or guide to the major employers and industries in the region. And when you're ready to begin your information interviews (see chapter 7), your library may be able to help you with local networking contacts. For example, at the Cuyahoga County Public Library in Maple Heights, Ohio, the InfoPLACE Career Information Center has initiated the "Winner's Circle" file, a list of people in various fields who have indicated that they are willing to share their expertise with career explorers who have attended library career workshops.

And be sure not to overlook the vast resources at your area college or university library, especially one that has a business school. The only catch is that non-students usually are not allowed to check out any books.

Generally speaking, in any public library, books that have an "R" on their spine—for Reference—cannot be checked out. In that case, you must do your reading and notetaking on the premises. However, copying machines are usually provided near the reference area, so you can make photocopies of the pages you need. Also keep in mind that large libraries often have one or more "circulating" copies of a popular reference book that can be borrowed. So if the book you need bears the dreaded R, ask if there is another "copy to go."

Some general tips: When you're looking at career books, keep an eye on the year of their publication. If the book was published more than three years ago —which means it probably was written four years ago—any discussion of employment outlook, salaries, and education or training requirements is likely to be outdated. Especially in occupational research, you want to be reading the most recent materials you can. In truth, *any* book is months old when it's published, so to be best informed, you must also review the major monthly and weekly trade magazines and newsletters, and the daily business press. Many of the career sourcebooks will tell you what those periodicals are.

As for trying to gauge the veracity of the career materials you read, look up the information about an occupation or field that you already know a lot about. If the book has advice and information you consider to be valid, you might take that as an indication that the facts about other fields are equally well researched.

The Cyberlibrary

But let's get back to that new technology to be found amid the bookshelves. Some nontechies (read: almost everybody) may think that using a CD-ROM database and being online are one and the same, but that's not the case. (A database, by the way, is simply a collection of related information in electronic form—either on a CD-ROM or in a huge mainframe computer somewhere.)

CD-ROMs are compact discs that look just like the audio CDs you buy in a music store. But a CD-ROM is "played" by a computer rather than a sound system. CD-ROM stands for "Compact Disc Read Only Memory," which means you can access (read) the information on the disc, but you cannot change it (by adding or deleting information). All you can do is read what's already there (and print out the results of your search). When the information on the disc is updated, usually monthly or quarterly, the library (or any other subscriber) is simply sent a new disc. Compact discs truly are a marvel of space-saving technology, because one can hold the equivalent of about 300,000 typewritten pages. The entire contents of multivolume encyclopedias often fit on a single disc.

Searching a database online, on the other hand, is an interactive, "real time" process. It means the computer you are using is "talking" to another remote computer over a telephone line (hence, online). It also means the meter is running—because online, time is money. The database vendor charges you (at an hourly rate and depending on several factors) for every minute you are connected to that remote database. Many large libraries will do an online search for you and get back to you with the hard copy results, and they may begin charging only after a certain point to cover their expenses. But any fees should be discussed up front. (An exception to online search costs: If the library has a university connection to the Internet, the search is usually free of charge.)

"Most libraries will set a limit, for example, that the first fifteen minutes' worth of search time or the first $20 of charged services are free," says George Needham of the Public Library Association. "Because librarians are trained in things like advanced Boolean searching (see "First-Timer Tip: Keys to Keyword Searching" on page 71) and know which databases to access and how to get around them, they know how to make the searches very inexpensive. If what you're looking for is in a high-priced database, they'll let you know first that a search probably will cost X dollars and ask if you still want to do it. But the librarian also may be able to point out that the information you want is actually on CD-ROM, in which case you don't really need to go online at all."

Generally speaking, though, a library will be more likely to provide CD-ROM databases rather than online searching simply because no "new" charges are involved after the library has borne the start-up costs of installing a CD-ROM system. That's why library patrons are usually not charged any fee to use a CD-ROM.

But just to confuse you, you should know that most CD-ROM databases are also available online, either individually or through a major commercial service such as CompuServe (see chapter 6). The online databases are updated more often, some of them even on a daily basis.

Besides the speed and convenience, a big plus in database searching is that you'll never again discover that the last page of the article is missing because someone tore out the "free offer" coupon on the other side.

What Databases Have to Offer

Whether they are online or CD-ROM, databases generally provide their information in three ways: bibliographic citations, abstract summary, or full text.

Bibliographic databases could be called "just the facts." Also referred to as *index* or *reference* databases, they provide only the basic reference information: the name of the publication and the date the article appeared, the article's title and author, and the relevant page numbers. With this knowledge, you then have several options for obtaining the article. You may be able to access a full-text CD-ROM that's been designed as a "companion" to the bibliographic one. For example, the Magazine ASAP database provides the full text of many of the titles indexed in its companion databases—Magazine Index Plus and General Periodicals Index (see InfoTrac listing on page 69). Or you can go to the library that carries the publication and read it there in the original hard copy, or ask that library to photocopy the article and send it to your neighborhood branch. You may be able to order the article directly from the magazine publisher. Or you could pay a document delivery service to mail or fax it to you.

Abstract databases provide all the bibliographic information plus a short summary (about 150 words) describing the main points covered in the article. In many cases, this is enough to tell you whether you want to see the whole story; it may turn out that the article is not what you thought it was about at all. Conversely, the statistic or news nugget you're looking for may be included in the abstract, so you already have the information you need.

Full-text databases provide, as the name implies, the complete text of the original article. But the operative word here is "text." The nontext or graphical elements such as pictures, charts, and graphs that may have accompanied the story generally are not reproduced. This might involve a loss of meaning or context, but most of the time the text alone is all that you need.

Though there are hundreds of databases available on CD-ROM and thousands available online, there are certain ones that are more likely to be found in a public library (as opposed to an academic or corporate library). The most common business reference CD-ROMs generally are from InfoTrac (from Information Access Company) or Proquest (from UMI). The name InfoTrac refers to a collection of many CD-ROM databases. Several libraries in your area may tell you they have InfoTrac, but they may not all have the same database, so check before you make the trip over.

The usual suspects for CD-ROM reference at a public library include the following.

From InfoTrac:

- *Business Index* (Public Edition). Designed specifically for public libraries, it provides indexes and abstracts of more than 700 business, management, and trade journals, plus indexes of *The Wall Street Journal* (U.S. and Asian editions), the financial section of *The New York Times,* and *The Financial Times of Canada.*

- *General BusinessFile.* Called a "megafile" by one reference librarian, this database incorporates everything in the Business Index (above) plus two other CD-ROMs: Company ProFile, which gives directory listings for more than 160,000 private and public companies, and Investext, which provides full-text investment reports of more than 11,000 companies. General BusinessFile is designed to be one-stop shopping for anyone doing marketing, career, or investment research.

- *General Periodicals Index.* This provides indexes and abstracts to 1,100 general interest, business, and academic publications over the last four years, plus two months' indexing of *The New York Times, The Wall Street Journal,* and *The Christian Science Monitor.* Topics covered include small business management, industry trends, and consumer surveys.

From UMI Proquest:

- *ABI/Inform.* This offers citations and abstracts of articles from more than 800 management, marketing, and general business journals. A career searcher would be able to find profiles on the executives of a particular company, as well as business and industry analysis and news about research and development. Coverage may go back five years or longer, depending on which version of the database the library has.

- *Newspaper Abstracts.* This offers abstracts and indexing on thousands of articles from nine major newspapers: *The New York Times, The Wall Street Journal, The Washington Post, The Chicago Tribune, The Christian Science Monitor, The Los Angeles Times, The Boston Globe, The Atlanta Journal Constitution,* and *USA Today.*

- *Periodical Abstracts.* There is also more than one version of this database, but even the smallest offers abstracts of several hundred general reference and business publications, including *Time, Rolling Stone, Ladies' Home Journal,* and the *World Press Review.*

There are, of course, many other databases that a library might have, including the CD-ROM versions of the venerable print reference indexes from H. W. Wilson Company. The Wilson Disc offerings include *Biography Index, Business Periodicals Index, Education Index, General Science Index,* and the *Readers' Guide to Periodical Literature.*

As for online databases at libraries, it is far beyond the scope of this book to even begin to discuss the thousands of options that are out there. Books whose sole subject is online research are available to check for further guidance. But your best bet may simply be to go to the nearest library, preferably its career center, and ask the reference librarian what they have to offer. If that branch can't do an online search for you, they'll know who can.

First-Timer Tip: Keys to Keyword Searching

Generally, but not always, CD-ROM or online database searching uses what's called Boolean logic: You link your keywords (if you have more than one) by using the words AND, OR, or NOT. For example, if you want to know about the job market for auditors, you might phrase a keyword search this way:

(hiring OR employment) trends AND auditors

Putting the parenthesis around "hiring OR employment" throws a wider net. You don't want to exclude articles that use the word "hiring" instead of "employment." This way, either word, if used with "trends" AND "auditors" will produce a match.

If you want to further narrow your search to discussions of the job market for auditors in your geographic region, you could phrase your keywords statement this way:

(hiring OR employment) trends AND auditors AND
(New England OR Massachusetts)

Using AND narrows a search; OR broadens it. NOT tends to be used less often but also can be useful to eliminate material that won't interest you or that you already know about. For example,

shoe manufacturers NOT Reebok.

Most libraries that offer a CD-ROM database generally have a list of user instructions mounted near the computer. But again, don't be embarrassed to ask the librarians for advice. Helping you to learn about your possible next job is part of *their* job description!

The Best Borrower Book List

The new technology at libraries is terrific, but computer stations and CD-ROMs will never replace the printed word, right up there on the shelf.

Practically every day's mail brings a library "new and improved" reference books that will tell you practically everything about practically anything. Career center and reference librarians have bibliographies that can list hundreds of books, but there are a select group that are reached for again and again. Here are some of their "supersources"—old and new—of basic information that will aid in your career exploration. It is a highly selective (and somewhat subjective) list that certainly cannot cover the universe of what's out there, but it's a good place to start.

RESOURCES ON CAREER AND BUSINESS RESEARCH

- *Help! My Job Interview Is Tomorrow!: How to Use the Library to Research an Employer* by Mary Ellen Templeton, published by Neal-Schuman, 1991

As the title implies, the author, a business reference librarian, cuts to the chase. She tells the reader where to go in the bookstacks and what to read in "the first fifteen minutes" or "the next half hour" for what she calls a "quick and dirty" hunt. In addition to the staples for checking on a large, publicly held corporation, she also covers the tougher ground of researching a small business and a private company, as well as nonprofits and government agencies.

- *Researching Your Way to a Good Job: How to Find and Use Information on Industries, Companies, Jobs, Careers* by Karmen N. T. Crowther, published by John Wiley & Sons, 1993

This is another useful guide to navigating the library and using its tools. The author, another business librarian, provides tips on where to look for information on a variety of company types, job-related information on other communities if you're thinking of relocating, and career guidance. A helpful "arrow chart" at the front asks what you want to know ("Is the company foreign owned?" "Need to check salaries?") and refers you to the relevant chapter.

- *Fiscal Directory of Fee-Based Research & Document Supply Services,* published by ALA Books, 1992

As mentioned above, there are many resources that can do computer searches for you, and this book tells you who and where they are. Copublished by the County of Los Angeles Public Library, the directory lists 440 fee-based services—including libraries, commercial information professionals, and even international sources—that do computer research and document delivery. The book is indexed by types of services offered, research subject specialties, and online services available. The book costs $65, so you might want to check to see if—what else?—a library near you carries it.

CAREER REFERENCE STAPLES, OLD AND NEW

- *Occupational Outlook Handbook,* 1994–95 Edition, published by the U.S. Department of Labor, biennial

Generally regarded as the bible of occupational information, virtually every library carries the *Handbook,* as do school and college libraries. Published every two years, it describes 250 occupations in detail and every profile includes the same informational categories: nature of the work, working conditions, employment (current picture, number employed in the job), training required and other qualifications, projected job outlook (currently through the year 2005), earnings, related occupations, and sources of additional information. Its helpful sibling is the magazine *Occupational Outlook Quarterly*. Because it is published four times a year, it can discuss changing trends and research between printings of the *Handbook*.

- *Encyclopedia of Business Information Sources,* Ninth Edition, published by Gale Research, biennial

Designed to be a first stop in a search for information on 1,500 business topics, ranging from a broad area such as corporate finance or a narrower subject like business ethics and social responsibility. The book provides a quick survey of publications, reference works such as directories and CD-ROM databases, sources for statistics, prices, and more. There is much cross-referencing, so if you want to look up "cellular telephones," you would find that all the material is listed in the book under "mobile telephone industry."

- *Directories in Print,* published by Gale Research, annual

Formerly called the *Directory of Directories,* it lists the directory for a particular industry, if one exists. For example, if your targeted field is public relations, you would be referred to *O'Dwyer's Directory of Public Relations Firms.*

- *Professional Careers Sourcebook: Where to Find Help Planning Careers That Require College or Technical Degrees,* edited by Kathleen M. Savage and Charity Anne Dorgan, published by Gale Research, 1992

This guide augments the information about the 110 professional careers included in the *Occupational Outlook Handbook*. The expanded profiles include more on job outlooks and salaries, directories of educational programs, expanded reference works, professional associations, certification agencies and exams, and scholarships and grants.

- *Vocational Careers Sourcebook: Where to Find Help Planning Careers in Skilled, Trade and Nontechnical Vocations,* edited by Kathleen M. Savage and Karen Hill, published by Gale Research, 1992

The 135 careers covered in this book do not require a college degree, though some type of training may be necessary. Fields include the service industries, construction, sales, and law enforcement.

- *Job Hunter's Sourcebook: Where to Find Employment Leads and Other Job Search Resources,* Second Edition, edited by Michelle LeCompte, published by Gale Research, 1993

A super resource, worthy of the several awards it has won as an outstanding reference work. Pegged more to the actual job search than the two Gale Research books already mentioned, but also valuable for those still exploring. The guide is divided in two sections. Part one provides sources of job-hunting information for 165 specific professional and vocational occupations—from accountant to aircraft mechanic, stockbroker to social worker. Of particular use to explorers would be the employer directories and networking lists, handbooks and manuals about that particular field, associations and organizations, lists of internships, and additional bibliographies.

Part two provides names of reference works, newspapers, magazines and journals, audiovisual resources, online database services, software, and other resources in twenty-four topics of overall interest to job seekers, such as résumé writing or interviewing skills, and special areas such as outplacement, career transitions, self-employment, working at home, and working part time.

- *Encyclopedia of Associations Volume 1, National Associations of the U.S.,* published by Gale Research, annual

This guide gives short descriptions of 22,000 professional, trade, and other nonprofit associations for hundreds of fields. You can get the address, telephone and fax numbers, contact names, the group's basic purpose and titles of its publications, and upcoming convention dates and locations. These groups are valuable to career explorers because they're generally happy to provide print materials about their group and the industry at large, and/or referrals to members in your area. This encyclopedia is usually shelved with its companion volume of regional organizations.

But just to confuse you, "Volume 1" actually is three big books: part one and part two for the association listings themselves, and part three for the Name and Keyword Index that tells you where to look for things in parts one and two.

RESOURCES ON CAREERS AND OCCUPATIONS

- *The Complete Guide for Occupational Exploration,* published by Jist Works, 1993

This book organizes the 12,000-plus jobs in the revised *Dictionary of Occupational Titles* to twelve "clusters" of major occupational categories, called *interest areas.* These include artistic, scientific, plants and animals, selling, and physical performing. The interest areas are then divided into sixty-six work groups, and again into 348 more specific subgroups of related jobs. The guide also cross-references these jobs by interest, training, school subjects, work values, leisure and home activities, and military occupational specialties. It's a very helpful and user-friendly book, with plenty of ideas for both career changers and entry-level workers.

- *Occu-facts: Information on 565 Careers in Outline Form,* published by Careers, Inc., biennial

Good for career explorers who are still looking into broad areas, this book presents one-page snapshots of 565 occupations. Each profile covers typical duties, working conditions, physical surroundings, physical demands, aptitudes and temperament needed, educational requirements, salary ranges, and further sources of industry information.

- *Career Directory Series,* edited by Bradley J. Morgan, published by Gale Research, 1993

A series of fifteen big directories, each of which includes essays by industry professionals on how to get started and what to expect on the job as well as further resource listings, such as associations and publications. The series includes the fields of performing arts; film and video; computing and software; health care (physicians and nurses, therapists, and allied professionals); radio and television; travel and hospitality; business and finance; newspaper, magazine, and book publishing; marketing and sales; public relations; and advertising. It also lists internship possibilities.

- *"Opportunities In....."* (Series), published by VGM Career Horizons, NTC Publishing

Each volume in this 145-title series, pegged more to the entry-level market, looks at the history of the field, current job outlook and future trends, educational or licensing requirements, salaries, professional organizations, and much more. Professional and vocational occupations are included.

- *Careers Without College* (Series), published by Peterson's, 1993, 1994

These books provide a quick and basic introduction to jobs that do not require a four-year college degree to get an entry-level position. The series currently includes fourteen career fields, including fashion, fitness, computers, music, health care, and sports. Each book profiles five occupations in the designated field.

RESOURCES ON COMPANIES AND EXECUTIVES

- *Million Dollar Directory,* published by Dun & Bradstreet Information Services

Helpful for getting basic information on private companies as well as publicly held ones, the first three volumes of this series alphabetically list 160,000 firms. Among other things, you can find out the address and telephone of corporate headquarters, division names and lines of business, annual sales volume, total number of employees, and names, titles, and functions of key officers. The fourth and fifth volumes cross-reference businesses by industry classification codes and geographic location.

Dun & Bradstreet is a major player in business reference, so you might also want to consult their other directories. Among them: *Directory of Service Companies* (including businesses in such fields as health services, accounting, public relations) and *America's Corporate Families* for information on a company's subsidiaries and divisions (if you get a job with them, it's good to know how far afield you might be transferred!).

- *Standard & Poor's Register of Corporations, Directors, and Executives,* published by Standard & Poor's Corporation, annual

Another bread-and-butter library reference, this comprises three volumes. The third is the index of company names and tells where to find information about them in the other two volumes. The first volume briefly describes the companies and what they do; the second volume gives biographical information on key executives and directors. (Once you know who they are, you can see if there are more extensive articles about them through the *Business Periodicals Index,* either in print or CD-ROM if the library has it.) The *Register* includes only major corporations; there are no listings for private companies.

- *Hoover's Handbook of American Business, 1995: Profiles of Over 500 Major U.S. Companies,* Fifth Edition, published by Reference Press, 1994

This annual guide is good for a quick introduction to these public and private companies, their history, and current performance in their fields. Industries range from aerospace and biotechnology to accounting and retailing. Written in a lively style, the one-page profiles contain overviews of their operations, company strategies, lists of products, top officers, and key competitors. The latter point is helpful if you're still considering an industry as a whole and have not yet targeted a particular company. It's indexed by industry, headquarters location, people, companies, and brand names.

- *Hoover's Handbook of Emerging Companies, 1995: Profiles of 250 of America's Most Exciting Growth Enterprises,* Second Edition, published by Reference Press, 1994

This guide chronicles the rise of the hottest growth firms—from brewers to waste disposal services, fast-food outlets to online services, and health care providers to software designers. It includes company overviews and histories, up to six years' of financial and employment data, and product lists and key competitors. If you're considering becoming an entrepreneur, this may provide you with some inspiration.

▼ ▼ ▼ ▼ ▼ ▼ ▼ ▼

There you were, innocently collecting print materials and downloading articles, and now they have taken over your living room.

Information Distillation— Or, How to Sift Through All That Stuff

The information you gather in your career research can be invaluable, but it can also be overwhelming. There you were, innocently collecting print materials and downloading articles, and now they have taken over your living room.

Obviously, not all of it will be of help to you, but you need to begin to sort it out. This could be as basic as making a folder for each career or occupation that you're interested in or using large index cards to summarize categories of information about each one.

For example, on each occupation's card (or separate sheet within a folder), you might put just a few words or sentences under each of the following categories:

- Education or training requirements
- Tasks and responsibilities (What skills will be required?)
- General working conditions (Will you work outdoors? on the road? all day in an office? What are the typical work locations?)
- Salary levels for entry-level and more experienced workers
- Employment outlook (Is the occupation growing or shrinking overall? What about in your region or city?)
- Any significant physical factors (e.g., heavy lifting goes well beyond construction trades; health workers such as paramedics frequently lift injured people, including those who are unconscious)
- Any other factors of importance or concern to you (Will the job require constant travel? long hours? daily deadline pressure? Does it offer good benefits? generous vacation time?)

To get the data to transfer to the index cards, have a highlighter pen in hand as you review job profiles such as those in the *Occupational Outlook Handbook*. (We assume you've made a photocopy of the profile; no marking up the library's copy!) For example, as you read the sections that describe each job's typical tasks and responsibilities, make particular note of the adaptive and transferable skills involved. Do you have them and, if so, do you want to use them again? Do you want to learn them?

For example, if you have the *Occupational Outlook Handbook* profile on photographers and camera operators, you would read about the required abilities and qualities such as creativity, imagination, reliability, artistic ability, patience, and close attention to detail. As George M. Needham of the Public Library Association suggests, "Scan for the words describing the job that you think also describe you."

Sniffing out clues that relate to your life or work values is a little tougher because most career guides don't get into much of an occupation's "psychological profile." However, you can look for references to the work being particularly demanding, high pressured or stressful, as is the case with commodities trading or broadcast news producing. If your values include plenty of time with your family and a steady 9-to-5 workday, these factors are important to note.

Finally, go high-tech in your notetaking and research if you can. If you have a portable laptop computer, take it along with you to the library. Then you can set up individual files on your computer for each career and type in your notes directly as you go through reference materials. You could even start an advantages/disadvantages file right there. Remember, a lot of directories and other reference publications must be used on site and cannot be checked out.

Freelance writer Catharine Henningsen always takes her laptop to the library, but she also points out that if you have a desktop PC at home, you can still use it without having to drag it out of the house.

"My library has a PC for public use that you're even allowed to install your own software on," she says. "So if you can take your own floppy disk to your library, you can insert it in the library's PC and type your notes onto it, then simply print them out when you get home."

Not to mention that you can walk right by the line at the photocopy machine.

Of course, if you love writing longhand on those yellow legal pads, go for it. Whatever works for you is fine. The point is to give all those facts and figures some framework and structure to make it easier to compare occupations—and that's what you're there for, right?

You and Your Modem: Researching in Cyberspace

YOU'VE BEEN SPENDING productive time at the library, reviewing print career resources, perhaps searching the CD-ROM databases and collecting lots of great material. If you can, you also might want to try another option—what might be called the library without walls. It's a place where the book or magazine you want has never been checked out, and it never closes. Welcome to cyberspace, as the online world is known.

Unlike the library, this world is not free—but using it as part of your career exploration can pay, in terms of time saved and the up-to-date quality of the information you can get.

Why, you ask?

1. *You save time.* Instead of spending hours poring over print indexes and directories to find a citation for a magazine article—only to discover that the library's copy is missing in action—you can spend literally only a few minutes at the computer. And on your home PC, you can do it twenty-four hours a day. (Libraries are terrific, but as far as we know, none stay open all night.)

2. *You get the latest information.* Printed library indexes, of course, cannot include references to articles that were published just a few days ago,

and even CD-ROMs are generally updated only on a monthly or quarterly basis. Some online databases are updated daily. Online also makes particular sense if you are researching industries that change rapidly, such as telecommunications or biotechnology.

3. *You can search a gold mine of information to zero in on only the nugget you need.* This is probably the single most valuable factor in doing research online. You can pinpoint the exact knowledge you seek through the relevant key words that define your subject. The database will scour hundreds or thousands of articles to find only those that meet your criteria.

Sound good so far? There is a catch, of course: You have to pay to belong to the major online commercial services, and—backing up a step—you need to own a personal computer (PC), a modem, and a telephone (see "First-Timer Tip: Making Connections" on page 87). If you don't, then you need to have a good friend who will let you "mooch" off them and borrow their equipment.

The World of Online Services

In this chapter, we'll take a look at these major services: CompuServe, Prodigy, GEnie, America Online, Delphi, and, in its own category, the much-talked-about Internet. These services are geared to meet all of your personal as well as professional needs. You can get business information and the latest news, and send quick and cheap electronic mail (E-mail), but you can also play games, talk about your hobbies and other interests, and network, network, network.

It was estimated in 1994 that about one-third of American homes had a PC, but only five percent of those were as yet "online." If you're in one of them, it's something of an advantage because career research is literally at your fingertips. And later on, when you are ready to launch your job hunt, you can also use these services to post your résumé or check online job listings in specific areas.

Computer expert and author Alfred Glossbrenner points out the appeal of going online: "You can basically assume that anything you want to know is online. Everything in the online world fits into one of two broad categories: communication or information." Glossbrenner adds that the value of being online is not just in the research and reference capabilities, but in the human give-and-take.

"You shouldn't just look for databases online; the special interest groups (SIGs) are the great unknown resource," he adds. "Their message boards and libraries have all kinds of good stuff in them" (see "Networking in Cyberspace," chapter 7). In short, says Glossbrenner, "Everyone should subscribe to at least one major system."

Already, many business people note that some colleagues *expect* you to have an E-mail address. As Peter H. Lewis reported in *The New York Times* in February 1994, "It is not uncommon today to see as many as six or seven different electronic mail addresses printed on a business card or letterhead." In other words, going online may be nifty in itself, but in your next job it may be necessary—part of the way you communicate and do business.

Fine, you say, but don't you need a degree in computer science first? Relax. The five major commercial services aren't just for techies. Their ease of use and visual appeal continues to increase, especially with quality graphic user interface—easy-to-use menus that allow you to simply "point and click" your way to what you want (as opposed to typing in laborious text commands). So let's take a closer look at what they have to offer.

▼ ▼ ▼ ▼ ▼ ▼ ▼ ▼

"If you want to find every reference to some company or person, the only way to do that is electronically. Searchability and scannability is the great advantage of looking for information online."

ALFRED GLOSSBRENNER
ONLINE EXPERT AND AUTHOR

Some generalities: The monthly fees listed here are what you pay simply to belong to the service. It usually includes access to a package of certain basic services, such as E-mail, news and sports, weather, and classified ads. Almost everything else is a pay-as-you-go extended service, meaning you are billed "connect time charges" at an hourly rate for the exact number of minutes you actually spend online. There also may be additional costs to use premium services, such as the hundreds of specialized databases. The good news is that your actual telephone connection to the service may be free or very low cost because you will likely be able to use one of the service's own telephone network local access numbers (called a "node").

Most services generally offer new subscribers some type of free trial period. And when you do sign up, there usually is a free "practice" area in which you can learn such things as the service's various commands and menus, how to post messages and reply to them on a message board, and how to download (receive) a library file or upload (send) a mail message.

A few more generalities: CompuServe and GEnie offer the most business and professional services because these people are their targeted membership. Prodigy and America Online have a broader range of subscribers, with Prodigy especially known as a family service. All offer an encyclopedia that is included in the basic services. Grolier's *Academic American Encyclopedia* is carried by CompuServe, Delphi, GEnie, and Prodigy, while America Online offers *Compton's.*

So here is a by-no-means comprehensive look at what each of the services can offer a career explorer. Because their capabilities are so vast, this can only give you a flavor of what you can find online. Additional resources listed at the end of this chapter can take you much further. All fees quoted were those in effect at the time of publication.

First-Timer Tip: Making Connections

To enter cyberspace, you need a computer, a telephone, and a device called a *modem*—which actually does the "talking" between two computers. The modem connects both to your computer and a telephone jack.

The most crucial factor about a modem is its speed, defined as "bits per second" (bps) or "baud rate." A few years ago, 2400 bps was considered speedy, but now it's the slow lane. Today, 9600 bps (or even 14,400) is preferred, though not all the commercial services can accommodate that higher speed. The higher the bps, the faster you can download (transfer files from the service to your computer) and thus save money, because you pay for each minute you're connected.

To use the services, you also need some type of communications software that manages how you receive and send information while you're online. On Prodigy and America Online, you must use their specialized software; on the others, a general program like Procomm Plus or Smartcom can be used. On CompuServe, you can "get in" with their own specialty communications package (called CompuServe Information Manager, or CIM), provided your computer is powerful enough to handle the graphics elements. It's not required to access the service, but using it makes navigating quicker and easier. If you're going to buy a new computer, chances are it will already come bundled with the communications software for one or more of these services.

THE MAJOR ONLINE SERVICES PLAYERS

- **CompuServe**
  CompuServe Inc.
  5000 Arlington Centre Boulevard
  Columbus, OH 43220
  Headquarters: 614-457-8600
  Telephone sign up: 800-848-8199
  Users: 2.3 million

Who's Online?

CompuServe, the largest online service, periodically surveys its membership. A recent survey revealed these demographics:

- *91 percent of members work in a business or profession; 23 percent are executives or officers*

- *45 percent have a home-based business, either as their primary place of employment or in addition to their regular job*

- *90 percent are male*

- *Median age is 41.3 years; 62 percent are between 25 and 44*

- *69 percent have at least a four-year college degree; 30 percent have a master's or a doctorate*

- *Average household income is $93,000*

Fees: $9.95 a month; connect-time rate is $4.80 an hour for access with 2400 bps, 9600 bps, or 14.400 kbps modems.

CompuServe is probably the best known of the online services because it has been operating since 1979. Many experts feel it offers the most for your money in terms of the sheer amount of information available. It has more than 600 SIGs (called *forums;* bulletin boards are called *message boards*). One-third of the forums are devoted to computer subjects (hardware and software), and dozens of others are career related. In general, when you join a forum (which simply means typing in your name and that you wish to become a member of that forum), you are encouraged to post a brief message outlining what you do, your location, what expertise you can offer, or what you'd like to know (see "Networking in Cyberspace," chapter 7).

Two general career-related forums are Working From Home Forum and Entrepreneurs Small Business Forum. Working From Home is run by Paul and Sarah Edwards, best-selling authors of several books on that subject. Their forum is targeted to full- or part-time self-employed people as well as salaried telecommuters. They offer a monthly newsletter, "Making It on Your Own," which can be downloaded. The forum library contains a wealth of files on starting a business and keeping it going—for example, information on how to start a day-care program in your home.

The Entrepreneurs Forum is targeted to small business owners—or those who would like to be—and the professionals who serve them, such as attorneys, accountants, marketing experts, and venture capitalists. This is the place to find a file on how to write a business plan, for example.

Job-related SIGs on specific fields include Legal Forum, for attorneys, paralegals, corrections officers, and anyone else interested in the law; the Safetynet Forum, for police officers, firefighters, and emergency medical workers; and Public Relations and Marketing Forum, which covers PR and communications in the public and private sectors. The Education Forum attracts all levels of teachers, and Computer Training and Computer Consultant Forums target anyone involved in the process of learning about computers. The professional forums, in particular, tend to generate very quick responses; it's not unusual to see that a query has prompted at least one reply within an hour of its posting.

> ▼ ▼ ▼ ▼ ▼ ▼ ▼
> *Having online access to local newspapers is of tremendous value if you're considering a relocation.*

Research sample: The Business Database Plus service is terrific for getting access to those publications and industry newsletters that no public library is going to stock. There are five years' worth of business and trade journals, such as *Adhesives Age* and one year's worth of "niche" newsletters like *Advanced Wireless Communications*. This is a premium service, charged at a $15 hourly rate plus $1.50 per article retrieval (when you download an article or "capture" it to a file as it scrolls across the screen). Imagine how sharp you would appear at an information interview if you've read the last several issues of the key industry newsletter beforehand.

Another excellent bet is Knowledge Index (KI), which offers 100 of the databases from the massive Dialog Information Service. KI offers a menu-driven search option that's geared to nonprofessional researchers such as students or career seekers like you. Here you'll find several of the Standard and Poor's business reference databases. There's a small catch: You can only access KI on evenings and weekends. The database costs $24 an hour, but if you look at it as 40 cents a minute, it seems less daunting. It's common to be able to conduct a search and retrieve articles in less than fifteen minutes.

CompuServe also has News Source USA, which provides full text of newspaper articles from more than fifty newspapers around the U.S. and eight major magazines (*People Weekly, Sports Illustrated, Time, U.S. News*

Are You Online Yet?

5.5 million users already are—and that doesn't even include the estimated 20 million people who log on to the Internet.

& World Report, Business Week, Forbes, Fortune, and *Money*). Having easy access to local newspapers is of tremendous value if you're considering a relocation; you could search the *Fresno Bee* or *Charlotte Observer* or *Orlando Sentinel* for articles relevant to the industry or companies there you have in mind (not to mention the real estate rental market).

For sheer depth, CompuServe has the IQuest service, which provides more than 800 databases in business, government, research, and even sports and entertainment. A premium service, all IQuest databases carry a hefty surcharge, so it's probably not the place to begin your learning curve for online searching. A very extensive discussion of IQuest and other CompuServe research offerings is in the book *Find It Online* (see "Resources on Online Services" later in this chapter).

- **GEnie**
  General Electric Information Service
  401 North Washington Street
  Rockville, MD 20850
  Headquarters: 301-251-6415
  Telephone sign up: 800-638-9636
  Users: 350,000
  Fees: $8.95 monthly, including four free hours, then $3 an hour nonprime time connect rate thereafter. (Access weekdays between 8 A.M. and 6 P.M. prime time is another $9.50 an hour.) Users with 9600 bps modems pay a $6 per hour surcharge at all times.

On GEnie, a SIG is called a *roundtable* (RT) and there are a couple hundred of them. The most obvious choices for a career seeker include the Home Office/Small Business Roundtable and its sibling, the WorkPlace Roundtable. A sampling of board subjects include job-hunting strategies, telecommuters, office services as a business, minority business, and making creativity pay (for writers, photographers, artists, and musicians). The WorkPlace *sysops*—the people who administer the roundtable—include a computer programmer and consultant, a personnel director, and a certified public accountant. Other career-related RTs include Education, Law, Medical, Law Enforcement, Home and Real Estate, Home Improvement, Aviation, Military, Photo and Video, and Writers.

GEnie's career and professional services also include "Dr. Job," whose weekly column answers some of the various career questions posted online. Dr. Job also provides many workplace tips and feature articles, such as surviving a career crash or the pros and cons of franchising.

Research sample: GEnie is second only to CompuServe in its database offerings. It provides a gateway (sort of an electronic bridge) to two of the biggest players. Dow Jones News/Retrieval (an extra-cost service) includes fifty databases containing company and industry news and information, such as Standard & Poor's Online, and full text of hundreds of national and regional publications. Career searchers can use Dow Jones to track the latest on firms that interest them, their financial records, and annual and quarterly reports. GEnie also offers virtually all of the 450 databases from Dialog, including *D&B U.S. Company Profiles,* the *Encyclopedia of Associations,* and *Marquis Who's Who.*

- **America Online**
  America Online, Inc.
  8619 Westwood Center Drive
  Vienna, VA 22182-2285
  Headquarters: 703-448-8700
  Telephone sign up: 800-827-6364
  Users: 1 million
  Fees: $9.95 monthly, including five hours connect time, then $2.95 an hour thereafter. (Rate applies 24 hours a day.)

▼ ▼ ▼ ▼ ▼ ▼ ▼ ▼

"Job hunters should introduce them- selves electronical- ly to employers by using an online résumé bank. A sizable number of companies are searching electron- ic résumé banks and not even advertising their job openings."

JAMES GONYEA
"CAREERDOC"
AMERICA ONLINE

America Online (AOL) is a fast-growing online ser- vice and is considered user friendly, largely due to its easy-to-understand graphics and plain-English instructions.

AOL's career-related SIGs, which may be called *clubs* or *forums,* include the Aviation Club, Business & Finance, Legal Special Interest Group, Desktop Publishing, Education (which includes areas specifi- cally for members of the American Federation of Teachers and the National Education Association), Emergency Response, Health Professionals Network, Nurses Network, Writers Club, Real Estate, and the National Professional Photography Association. The Microsoft Small Business Center is a useful source of business articles on starting up and running a busi- ness, and a calendar of upcoming seminars in various fields is also posted. As with the SIGs on the other ser- vices, the libraries are rich resources of thousands of articles and reports that can be downloaded.

AOL can boast that it offered the first online career and employment guidance agency, the Career Center. In addition to such services as a career resource library, an employment agency database, a résumé tal- ent bank, and a college financial aid service, the cen- ter includes the services of "CareerDoc" James Gonyea, a Florida psychologist and career counselor who conducts private online counseling sessions with career seekers and job hunters at no additional cost. He or an associate also respond to questions posted to the Ask the Counselor bulletin board or sent by E- mail. In addition, the Career Center offers a database of 225 occupational profiles derived from the *Occupational Outlook Handbook.*

Research samples: AOL has the online version of *Hoover's Handbook of American Business,* a source of company overviews and histories. If you need to know the very latest on a topic, say, you have an informa- tion interview today and the company is in the news, AOL offers News Search. This database of news stories is updated continuously, so you could find out something before Peter Jennings tells you tonight. That plus is also a drawback, though, for files are kept for less than a week. If you need a lengthier research history, you need another database. If you're interested *only* in news stories about the latest developments in the computer industry, then AOL offers the continuously updated NewsBytes database.

- **Prodigy**
  Prodigy Services Company
  445 Hamilton Avenue
  White Plains, NY 10601
  Headquarters: 914-448-5200
  Telephone sign up: 800-PRODIGY
  Users: 2 million
  Fees: $9.95 monthly, including five hours connect time, then $2.95 an hour.

Reflecting its emphasis on a family membership, the majority of the fifty bulletin boards on Prodigy are targeted to hobby and leisure interests. The most appropriate board for career searchers is the Careers Board. In mid-1994, discussion topics here included career change, relocating, accounting, airline, arts and entertainment, court reporting, design and construction, engineering, entrepreneurs, insurance, legal, medical/veterinary, sales and retail, management, police, fire, civil service, communications, computers, and consulting. Job seekers who already know what they're looking for can post a message describing themselves and their job target in the "position wanted" discussion area of the Career Board.

Other career-related bulletin boards are Office, International Business, Education, and Money Talk.

Research samples: As once described in a computer publication, Prodigy is the online service for the middle American family. As such, its emphasis is on leisure and sports and shopping services rather than the high-level research databases. It does have updated business and stock market news, but the career explorer probably will find the most usefulness in the bulletin boards mentioned above.

- **Delphi**
  Delphi Internet Services Corporation
  1030 Massachusetts Avenue
  Cambridge, MA 02138
  Telephone sign up: 800-695-4005 (voice)
  800-695-4002 (modem)
  Users: 100,000
  Fees: $10 monthly, including four hours connect time, then $4 an hour thereafter.

In size comparison to the other commercial services, Delphi is a midget, but it's poised for growth. It has 150 SIGs, called *groups, clubs,* or *forums,* and there's even the opportunity to create your own "custom forum" if what you're looking for doesn't exist.

Of those that already do, the career-related ones include Aviation SIG, Business Forum, Nurses, Desktop Publishing, Photography/Video Forum, Writers Group, Inventors/Inventions, and Telecommunications (two of the "custom" forums run by Delphi members themselves).

As of mid-1994, Delphi's main claim to fame among the five commercial services was that it was the only one providing full access to the Internet, although that will almost certainly change as the others get up to speed. Delphi has hundreds of online "moderators" to guide subscribers navigating the Internet, categorizing and arranging the data available.

Research samples: Delphi also provides access to all the databases on Dialog, but because it lacks the helpful search menus that one gets from GEnie or CompuServe, any bumbling around can get very expensive. If you are involved in health services or have a particular interest in AIDS information, Delphi offers (as part of its basic fee) the CAIN database, which stands for Computerized AIDS Information

Network. This database culls more than 3,000 sources from general interest and medical journals, as well as government sources. Parts of CAIN are updated daily, and it is available only on Delphi.

- **The Internet**

Just within the last year or so, it seems, everybody wants to get on the Internet—or the Net, as it is known—even if they aren't terribly sure what exactly it is. If you're one of them, you should know that the Internet is *not* a consumer-oriented, highly organized service like the five just discussed. It's been around for twenty-five years, but has been something of a closed society—the domain of government and military agencies, universities, research centers, and other users who understood its complex ways.

No more. Current estimates are that 20 million people on 25,000 computer networks in 135 countries already have access to the Internet, with 150,000 more coming on each month. But nobody knows the numbers for sure. No one actually owns the Internet, and no single company or authority officially runs it. There is no "there" there, because it's everywhere. This is sort of a good news/bad news scenario, because the lack of a central organization often means a certain degree of chaos. Novice adventurers have written of trying to find a certain database or newsgroup, only to somehow find themselves "at" the University of Singapore.

As writer Laurie Flynn observed in a *New York Times* "Executive Computer" column, "To the uninitiated, navigating the Internet can feel like sailing the Pacific without a chart or compass. Users may reach land eventually, but whether it's their intended destination is another matter."

Their intended destination is probably one or more of the estimated 10,000 discussion areas or "newsgroups" on what's called the Usenet. To be sure, hundreds of these are on somewhat arcane, if not bizarre,

> ▼ ▼ ▼ ▼ ▼ ▼ ▼ ▼
> *No one actually owns the Internet, and no single company or authority officially runs it. There is no "there" there, because it's everywhere.*

subjects, but there are many career-related news-groups, too. Some topics include operating your own business, contract labor, employment and careers in general, jobs offered and jobs wanted, mechanical engineering, careers in scientific research, para-medics, technical writing, home economics and career education, and industrial arts and vocational education.

Today you can "get on" the Net through one of many commercial providers (if you aren't already con-nected through your current employer or have access through a university). You pay a fee to be connected—usually around $15 or $20 a month and a low hourly connect time, but once you're there, everything's free. Unlike the commercial services, there are no charges for accessing databases or posting to the newsgroups.

There are many new books that introduce you to the workings of the Internet in great detail, though it's such a rapidly changing universe that magazines can barely keep up. If you want to learn more, start read-ing periodicals such as *Internet World,* or look for relat-ed articles in the major computer magazines.

Here are some of the career-related services on the Internet:

- Online Career Center
  317-293-6499
- Career Connections
  415-903-5800

For a service provider in your region and more information about the Internet, you can call the InterNIC Information Services at 800-444-4345.

The closest thing to an authority for the Internet is this volunteer group:

The Internet Society
1895 Preston White Drive, Suite 100
Reston, VA 22091
703-648-9888

RESOURCES ON ONLINE SERVICES

- *Find It Online!* by Robert I. Berkman, published by Windcrest/McGraw-Hill, 1994

As he previously did with library CD-ROM collections, here Berkman also goes into great detail about what you can find online and where. In particular, he gives extensive descriptions of all the five online services discussed here and much more detail about their research databases.

- *The Little Online Book: A Gentle Introduction to Modems, Online Services, Electronic Bulletin Boards, and the Internet* by Alfred Glossbrenner, published by Peachpit Press, 1994

- *Internet Slick Tricks* by Alfred and Emily Glossbrenner, published by Random House, 1994

- *The Complete Handbook of Personal Computer Communications,* Third Edition, by Alfred Glossbrenner, published by St. Martin's Press, 1990

- *Glossbrenner's Master Guide to GEnie* by Alfred Glossbrenner, published by Osborne McGraw-Hill, 1991

If you start to get into the online world, at some point you will want to read Glossbrenner. He has the gift of writing in plain English and often wittily about complex subjects. The first two books listed above are pegged to cyberspace novices and are designed to help cut through the online fog. The *Complete Handbook* covers just about everything you can do with your PC. The GEnie guide is a tad outdated because GEnie's price structure and some services have changed, but the crux of what it can offer has not. If GEnie will be your choice of online service, this guide can be of assistance.

- *CompuServe from A to Z: The Ultimate CompuServe Reference* by Charles Bowen, published by Random House Electronic Publishing, 1994

An exhaustive guide to the services, people, and ideas available on CompuServe and where to find them. It offers good hand-holding for beginners, and there's always something new to learn, even for more experienced users.

- *Electronic Job Search Revolution* by Joyce Lain Kennedy and Thomas J. Morrow, published by John Wiley & Sons, 1994

When you are ready to job hunt, cyberspace is ready for you. This timely book explains how to conduct a job search online—from résumé services to classified ad companies to employer databases to a list of information brokers who can do all the digging for you on how to target companies that meet your preferred specifications. Kennedy also has written a companion book, *Electronic Resume Revolution.*

- *The Online Job Search Companion: A Complete Guide to the Resources Available Via Your Computer* by James C. Gonyea, published by McGraw-Hill, 1994

The newest online job-seeking guide, this book also includes a floppy disk with software for one free month of access to America Online's Career Center, which is run by "CareerDoc" Gonyea.

Career Profile • Career Profile • Career Profile

The Path of a Career Explorer: One Story of Career Researching

Here's an example of how a fictional career changer— we'll call her Donna—might in real life go about doing her preliminary print and online research on targeted careers, and how she would weigh information she's gathering about those occupations against the important factors she identified through her self-assessment process.

Career Profile • *Career Profile* • *Career Profile*

Donna is twenty-five, has a bachelor's degree in liberal arts and has been working in public relations for the travel industry since she graduated from college. She basically fell into her job because a friend of the family owned the public relations agency she went to work for. And though there are fun elements to her job—the free trips to expensive resort hotels being one of them—lately she has been increasingly dissatisfied with her work. She wants to have a little more meaning in her day, a more tangible sense that she has done something directly to improve someone else's life.

Donna has taken the *Strong* and learned that she has a dominant Social code, followed by Artistic and Realistic. She also took the MBTI inventory, which revealed that she is an ESFJ, with decided preferences on the Sensing and Feeling scales. People of this type are known to enjoy work that provides practical help and service to people, and they do well in health-related professions and community service.

On her work values exercise in chapter 4, Donna's primary values include helping others in a direct way and having a lot of day-to-day contact with the public. Her life values encompass responsibility, using imagination in problem solving, and a sense of accomplishment. Of her functional skills, Donna's preferences include counseling or advising people, or motivating them.

Because her sister is a registered nurse who works in a hospital, Donna has been exposed to many of the allied health professions. Over the last several months she has begun to consider two of them: occupational therapist (OT) and medical social worker. She already knows that either choice will mean going back to school for up to two years, either to get a certificate in OT or a master's in social work.

Here's what she learns about each career after doing research.

Career Profile • Career Profile • Career Profile

Occupational Therapy

Like most career explorers, Donna heads first for the library. She selects career guidebooks such as the *Occupational Outlook Handbook* and the *Career Information Center* and reads all the segments about occupational therapy. She also checks out *Opportunities in Occupational Therapy Careers,* one of the series published by VGM Career Horizons.

In the *Encyclopedia of Associations,* she locates the American Occupational Therapy Association (AOTA) and calls them for their basic packet of career information. In all of these materials, Donna learns that OTs work one-on-one with their patients to help them overcome physical disabilities from illness or injury, or to better cope with developmental disabilities or physical changes due to advancing age. Typical patients are people who must relearn basic self-care skills after a stroke or accident, or children who have cerebral palsy. The OT's goal is to help them all become as self-sufficient and productive as possible. Because Donna considers herself empathetic, a good listener, and an effective problem solver, her interest in this occupation continues to increase.

Donna has some concerns about the science study that would be required in going back to school, but finds it less threatening than she thought would be the case. She reads that coursework includes anatomy, physiology, and kinesiology, as well as courses like applied arts, recreation, and home economics. She learns that an OT might teach crafts such as leatherwork to help patients improve muscle strength or range of motion, or get patients involved in music or art activities to help them express how they feel. This sounds appealing, and one of her hobbies is painting.

Donna also likes the idea that she'd be part of a rehab team—working with the patient's doctor, nurses, perhaps a physical therapist, a speech pathologist or

Career Profile • *Career Profile* • *Career Profile*

recreational therapist, and an OT assistant, as well as consulting with the patient's family when appropriate.

As much as possible, Donna also wants to ascertain that she's choosing a field with excellent job prospects. She reads that occupational therapy is one of the fastest growing occupations; according to the U.S. Bureau of Labor Statistics, there will be a 55 percent increase in the number of positions over the next decade. She learns that one-third of OTs work in hospitals, while another 20 percent work in schools and 13 percent in rehab hospitals or centers. Some OTs specialize in areas such as pediatrics, gerontology, or mental health. Donna thinks she'd enjoy working primarily with children.

Browsing through several issues of the newspaper *OT Week* at the local college's library, she is impressed by the pages and pages of help wanted ads. There is great flexibility in this career; she could work all over the country on short-term assignments if she chose. But she prefers a structured schedule and likes the idea that most workweeks are a standard forty hours with predictable appointments. Generally, there is no evening or shiftwork, even in a hospital setting. This is favorable, because she currently works several evenings a month at client-related functions and wants her evenings to be free in her next job.

Though a starting salary would likely be in the mid-20s, the potential for earning a salary in the '30s within a few years is great. In fact, according to a brochure she received from the AOTA, half of all the new occupational therapists earned an average of $34,500 in their first positions.

In addition to her print research, Donna asked a friend who has accounts on the GEnie and CompuServe computer services for a little help. On GEnie's Medical Bulletin Board, there is a topic for occupational therapists and those interested in the field. Donna posted a query asking what personal traits are necessary for success in occupational therapy and any other advice people could offer about the career. The subsequent replies included a comment from the mother of an autistic child, who felt an OT should be warm and relaxed, very patient, and aware that there won't be immediate results, but "comfortable asking for just a little more than they did the time before."

Another reply noted that pay could be higher and that the field is a younger one and not as well established as physical therapy or registered nursing. The person summarized that, rather than trying to mend broken bones, an OT tries to help a person with a disability live a satisfying life by being able to get dressed in the morning, make breakfast, go to work, and interact with people. Donna recognizes this as the holistic approach that appeals to her about the work, and once again feels she's on the right track considering this career.

Because she already has a BA, Donna wants a school that offers a post-BA certificate program. However, fewer than a dozen schools around the country offer such programs, and since she doesn't want to relocate at this time, this will be a factor in her ultimate career choice.

In summary, in an OT career, Donna sees challenge matched by reward and is confident that she could find whatever she wanted in the job market, given the demand for people. She looks forward to setting up some information interviews through her sister's medical contacts and by calling hospital and clinic OT departments directly.

Career Profile • Career Profile • Career Profile

Medical Social Work

The other career that strongly appeals to Donna is that of social worker. This is a much broader universe than OT and offers dozens of possible work environments.

To begin her research, Donna reads several occupational profiles in the career guides listed earlier. She learns there are three basic areas of social work: individual casework, group work, and community service work. She's thinking in terms of hospital-based medical social casework, which means directly helping patients and their families cope with illness and deal with problems that may affect recovery or rehabilitation. In this role, she might comfort a parent who is distraught over the premature birth of a child or ensure that another patient understands and follows medication recommendations.

Of increasing importance in this job, she would also help plan and coordinate a patient's needs after discharge from a hospital, such as arranging for at-home services from meals-on-wheels lunch delivery or obtaining a wheelchair. This is one reason growth is expected in this area; the financial pressures to quickly discharge patients from hospitals means that more activities must be coordinated before they return home. The work also involves collaborating with a patient's doctor and other health professionals involved with their care.

An M.S.W. would require very little science coursework, which Donna considers a point in its favor. A master's program would take about two years to complete, and her choice of schools would be greater than with the OT certificate programs. At the library, she also does a CD-ROM search of the Periodicals Index and prints out full text of a few recent newspaper features about the changing roles of the hospital social worker's job. She also reviews the book catalog and

Career Profile • Career Profile • Career Profile

checks out several titles on social work to get a broad overview of the field.

She also again uses her friend's computer to access CompuServe and the Magazine Database Plus service, where a search for articles about social workers yields a long magazine piece about options in social work careers, which she downloads for a charge of $1.50.

And at a local college library that stocks many health-related publications (because the college has a nursing school), Donna looks over several issues of *Social Work* and *Health and Social Work*, two journals from the National Association of Social Workers (NASW) that she found listed in the Social Worker profile in the *Job Hunter's Sourcebook*. She finds topical issues in the monthly newspaper *NASW News* and sees that there are also listings of job openings, though they are predominantly in smaller cities or outlying areas.

In literature she requested from the NASW, Donna reads that salaries for social workers are all across the board, ranging by geographic location, experience, setting, and duties involved. Though she would likely earn a starting salary in the mid-20s, the NASW reports that a social worker with an M.S.W. can expect an annual income ranging to about $40,000. Of one thing they are sure: The demand for social workers is on the rise. According to the Bureau of Labor Statistics, by the year 2000 there will be more than half a million social workers, up from 484,000 in 1992.

Donna learns that about 40 percent of social workers are employed by government agencies at the state, county, and city level, which means they are subject to funding cuts and staff reductions. However, turnover is high in this field because of burnout. Though some urban areas have an abundance of social workers, creating a great deal of competition for these jobs, opportunities are increasing in the home health care field.

Career Profile • *Career Profile* • *Career Profile*

Donna admits that she has some concern about the "downside" of the social worker's job—the tragedy of some clients' lives and the inability of anyone to solve everyone's problems. In one of her articles, she read that a hospital social worker might have to deal with a sick grandparent abandoned in a hospital emergency room or a teenager shot in gang violence. Donna reads that emotional maturity and a genuine desire to help people are nonnegotiable requirements for this type of work, and she feels that she qualifies on both counts and could meet the challenge of the job.

In this field, especially in a hospital setting, she could generally count on working five days a week for an eight-hour day, with only an occasional need for overtime.

Finally, Donna bugs yet another friend, this one a subscriber to America Online, to E-mail the Career Center's "CareerDoc" James Gonyea for some additional advice. In addition to sending an occupational profile and having the option of online consultation, Dr. Gonyea makes these suggestions: Search the online college database for schools offering social work programs and contact their career planning advisers to ask questions about the occupation; then go into the "Help Wanted USA" database, search for social worker listings, then contact the human resources departments of those agencies or hospitals offering positions and ask what they'll be looking for two years from now.

In either of her targeted careers, Donna would need to pass an exam and be licensed to practice in her state. She thinks she's leaning toward the OT choice, but in both cases she starts making a list of questions to ask during information interviews. Because of her diligent research, her questions are bound to be smart ones.

Going to the Source: Networking Your Way to Your Next Career

7

AT THIS POINT in your occupational fact hunt, you're probably knee-deep in secondary sources of career materials, such as books and trade journal articles and newspaper clips and pamphlets from professional associations. You're probably even confused. Is what that book said a year ago about the managed-care health industry still true? And what about the two huge retailers that just announced a merger—what's that going to mean now in terms of their employment picture or their advertising agencies?

So now is the time to start sorting things out by going to a primary source: real people. You're going to start networking. Despite rumors to the contrary, there is absolutely no mystique or secret to the networking process. It means only this: talking to people to both get and give information.

In this chapter, we will discuss networking in terms of the information interview, also called a *research interview* or *fact-finding interview*. In the career search process, once you've identified the career areas that suggest a good fit, it's time to start talking to the people who are already doing what you think you'd like to do. It's also a first step in the process of reality testing your choice (more on that in chapter 9). Information interviewing helps you find out what an industry and/or a particular occupation is really like right now.

> ▼ ▼ ▼ ▼ ▼ ▼ ▼ ▼
>
> *The U.S. Department of Labor estimates that 80 percent of all jobs are filled through personal contacts.*

And though it's not mysterious, it does take time and effort. It means creating your own personal directory of contacts in order to target someone who's working in the type of job that interests you.

As career counselors will tell you, it is vital to find out whether a career is truly everything you think it is, *before* you invest big money in returning to school or relocating (say, before you leave Kansas City to pursue marine biology in San Diego). Though initially disappointing, it is extremely helpful if you find out that your dream job would—for your particular skills and interests—actually be a dud.

Networking should be a win-win scenario—helpful to both parties. Yet in recent years, some business people have felt abused by networkers. There have even been variations on jokes such as the following:

> Which message is a busy executive's worst nightmare?
>
> A. Mike Wallace of *60 Minutes* is here, and he won't leave until he asks you about those shredded documents.
>
> B. A networker wants to meet with you.

The major public relations problem networking suffers from is that many contacts have given too many information interviews only to discover that the person interviewing them is really trying to get a job right away, preferably with the contact's company. Some critics even say that the whole idea of networking has become passé, but most career counselors and business people strongly disagree. Done properly, there simply is no better way to get the accurate, up-to-date, hands-on information you need to make a truly informed choice of a career—not to mention a job further down the line. The U.S. Department of Labor estimates that 80 percent of all jobs are filled through personal contacts.

Nevertheless, career counselors often report that many clients—whether they're twenty-one or forty-one—can be intimidated at the prospect of asking strangers for career advice. Some are reluctant to seem "needy" or uninformed. Older workers, in particular, can sometimes feel awkward, especially if they find themselves in the position of asking twenty-three-year-olds for help. "People are concerned about 'using' other people, but all of us really like to be helpful to others if it doesn't cost us too much," observes Nancy Pool Dixson, director of the Career Center at the University of Denver.

So what can informational interviewing do for you? Many things:

- *It gives you a sense of control over your career research because all the initiative comes from you.* You're the one with the list of questions, so you control the discussion. Unlike a job interview, *you* are interviewing the contact, not vice versa.

- *It helps clarify and verify your career choice.* To get what you need to know, you have to be focused. As your knowledge grows with each interview, you reassess and refine your goal. Because you are getting firsthand information, it should either confirm your career selection or rule it out—and, with any luck, point you in a better direction.

- *It boosts your self-esteem.* As two interviews become five and then ten, your nervousness fades and your confidence rises. You'll be more articulate and less reliant on your original "script" to get you through each call. This can't help but improve your general ability to approach and converse with people you don't know (remember the last function where you felt so uncomfortable because you didn't know anyone in the room?).

> ▼ ▼ ▼ ▼ ▼ ▼ ▼ ▼
>
> *The value of networking is connecting and cross-pollinating with ever larger circles outside your own.*

- *It helps you make favorable contacts in a career area for the future—and possibly long-term friends.* As noted earlier, most people get their jobs with the help of someone they already know. And even if a new contact is not a key player in your career search, she or he may well become a personal friend.

Where to Find Contacts

Beginning writers are often told that the first rule is "write what you know." To paraphrase that advice, the first rule of networking would be "ask who you know." Don't be concerned because you want to find out about meteorology and everyone in your family is in landscaping. It's been said a million times: You never know who can help you. A wonderful lead may come from the most surprising source. The value of networking is connecting and cross-pollinating with ever larger circles outside your own. So even if your first circle—family and friends—does not include someone in your targeted career, that circle will grow exponentially. People know people who know people—one of whom will know the exact person you should call.

When you stop to think about it, you almost won't believe how many people you already know. Your initial list of contacts would include:

- Immediate family, extended relatives, and their friends and relatives (If you're out of practice or especially shy, it's always helpful to start calling people who love you—or at least know you.)
- Your personal friends (and all *their* relatives)
- Members of your religious affiliation and its clergy
- Other parents at your children's school and the school's teachers and staff
- Colleagues in civic and service organizations (e.g., Rotary, Kiwanis, Junior League)

- Service providers (your doctors, dentist, attorney, accountant, auto mechanic, manicurist, insurance agent, hairdresser, travel agent, florist, dry cleaner, real estate broker, and letter carrier)

- Fellow sport, hobby, and fitness buffs (bowling league, bridge group, quilting club, health club); don't forget the people who sit next to your subscription seats at the theater/opera/symphony, baseball/football stadium, or basketball arena

- Members of your current trade group or professional association; no one was issued their career at birth, so it's likely that your associates have worked in other industries (if you're planning to change careers)

- Former teachers, college professors, and school and college classmates

- Former office colleagues (current ones can be tricky unless you're one of many workers being outplaced, in which case your career search is common knowledge)

- Your college alumni office; even if your diploma is twenty-five-years-old, they will tell you if there are any alumni in your region working in the field that interests you

- Other trade organizations (they can put you in touch with local chapters and tell you about area seminars, conventions, or workshops; the *Encyclopedia of Associations* is a fabulous resource for locating these groups)

- The local chamber of commerce (a veritable fountain of information about the businesses in your area and their key personnel)

- The local telephone *Yellow Pages,* especially the "Business to Business" version—an obvious, yet often overlooked source

If you have lost your job, career counselors encourage you to also take advantage of job support groups for the unemployed or those in career transition. In addition to providing practical guidance and emotional support, such groups offer excellent networking opportunities. Many churches and community groups often sponsor such clubs. Check in your local newspaper's business or community events pages for possible listings. Also, the *National Business Employment Weekly* newspaper (published by *The Wall Street Journal* and found at most major newsstands) has a weekly "Calendar of Career Events" featuring free or low-cost job clubs and other networking groups around the country.

Making Contact

For everyone you contact, your message is simple: "I'm considering a career in X field. Do you know anyone I could talk to who does that type of work?" That's the person with whom you want to arrange an information interview.

If you'd prefer to make your initial contact on paper rather than over the phone, your script could read something like the career changer's on the following page.

Of course, when you say you will call, *call*. There is a special place in hell for people who say they are going to do something and then do not. Besides, if you can't follow through on your *own* projects, what does that say about your ability to commit to someone else's—such as a future employer's?

February 21, 1995

Ms. Debra Wagner
Vice President
Marketing Insights, Inc.
Chicago, IL 12345

Dear Ms. Wagner,

Mark Smith of Marketing Insights, Inc., suggested that I contact you about a career change I'm considering. After fifteen successful years as a manager in human resources, I have been exploring options in sales and marketing. Before I proceed any further, I'd appreciate an opportunity to meet with you to get your advice about such a move.

I will call your office on Thursday morning, the 28th, to find out if and when I might be able to arrange a twenty-minute appointment with you.

Sincerely,
Louis Tyrell

First-Timer Tip: Package Yourself Professionally

Unless you're considering a career in graphic design and you make your own paper from wood pulp, it's best to keep your personal stationery simple and elegant: a high-quality white or ivory cotton bond paper with matching envelope. (We know of one chief executive officer who personally checks mail from career seekers to see if the envelope matches the paper, if the address is typed or at least neatly printed in dark ink, and if the stamp is on straight.) And speaking of stamps—use them. *Never* run your personal mail through your current employer's postage meter. In terms of the total image projected, be aware that such small details are a big factor to many business people.

If you can't afford engraved stationery, or if your address may be changing, any computer-owning friend with word processing or desktop publishing software can quickly make you a nice-looking letterhead, with your name, home address, and telephone and/or fax number. Once you have a good quality printout, then you can inexpensively reproduce that master copy on decent paper at a local copy center.

For Information, Dial Direct

To get the quickest results, targeting your sources by telephone can't be beat. Again, if you have your pitch outlined, you're less likely to sound nervous or tentative when you call. Here's a sample script for a soon-to-be graduate:

Good morning, Mr. Lindsey, my name is Ron Burmingham. Deandra Wright suggested I call you. I will be graduating in June from Georgetown University with a major in economics and I'm considering a career in finance.

If you have a moment, I'd like to set up an information interview with you to discuss the financial assistant position.

If you have time next week, I was hoping we might meet for twenty minutes at your convenience. I'd truly appreciate it if we might set something up.

Before you get off the phone, be sure you have the correct address (never assume they haven't moved since the telephone book was printed). Ask for the contact's direct phone number. Sometimes the direct number can be reached when the switchboard is closed (these days, many firms offer twenty-four-hour voice mail), which can be important if you're meeting someone before or after regular office hours and an emergency or other problem arises that causes a last-minute change in your plans.

Even if you have a notebook full of personal refer-rals, at some point you may have to make a cold call—writing or calling someone you don't know and for whom you do not have a personal contact. Keep in mind that cold calling is what people such as salespeo-ple and stockbrokers do for a living—so you certainly can do it for the short term. Even so, any conversa-tional bridge is helpful, so if you saw the contact quoted or mentioned in a recent trade magazine or journal, mention it.

"You should be reading the trade journals—not only is it an appropriate reference to make when you call, but it also shows that you're serious about this," observes Les Garnas, a sales and marketing trainer and author of a book on networking. "You want to be flattering in an appropriate way; your research has shown you that this is someone you should be talking to. You've done your homework, but there's this miss-ing piece—and that's why you need to talk to this per-son. In information interviewing, you're not looking for the obvious—you're looking for things that aren't written down anywhere."

But how does a cold caller get past the "gatekeeper"—the person who screens calls for the great source? If you are a born silver-tongued schmoozer and can pull

Cold Calls
Can Pay Off

JoAnn Kroll, director of Career Planning and Placement Services of Bowling Green State University in Ohio, recalls this example of information interviewing and cold calling:

"Bowling Green has for-credit classes in which students go through the whole process of career decision making. In one step, they talk to someone who has the job they aspire to hold. I'll never forget a sophomore who wanted to go into public relations. He got the number for Goodyear from the telephone directory, reached the switchboard operator, and said, 'I have some correspondence for the vice president of public relations. May I have the correct spelling of that person's name and specific title?' He got it, called back five minutes later, got through to the man, and asked for half an hour of his time.

"So he went out to Goodyear. Well, he'd done his homework, he had a good sense of what PR people did, and, of course, he was highly complimentary about the blimp! The vice president wound up spending half a day with him. The VP told the student to stay in touch, and he ended up getting an internship with Goodyear the following summer."

it off, pure charm may work, but most people are better served by straightforward honesty. A good approach is to try and make the call screener an ally in your project.

You might say something like,

Ms. Morris, my name is Ellen Whitfield. I realize your boss is extremely busy, but I know that she is one of the best-known experts in this area, and I'd really value her input about my career research. I wouldn't need more than a few minutes of her time, and I don't want to take more of yours by bothering you with repeated phone calls. When do you think I'd have the best chance of reaching her?

To that end, a couple of caveats:

- *Don't alienate the gatekeeper.* Displaying a high-handed or imperious attitude with the assistant who answers your target's telephone will be shortsighted, indeed. Any caller—*especially* one seeking advice and assistance—should be gracious to the person who has the power to grant or deny access to the contact. This should, of course, be common sense, but, as it's often been observed, common sense ain't so common.

- *Don't attempt false familiarity.* Asking the assistant to put "Jerry" on the line or saying that you're "returning Jerry's call" might get you connected. But how will you handle a less-than-friendly reaction when "Jerry," who, it never fails to turn out, is always called "Gerard," picks up the phone and realizes he doesn't know you? Even though some career guides do suggest that networkers try some of the verbal sleight-of-hand that salespeople may use to get through to prospects, don't do it. For every person who might be impressed by your cleverness or ingenuity, many others will be extremely irritated. Why take the chance?

Where should you meet your contact? Obviously, whatever is best for them is what you'll agree to, but if you do meet at their workplace, the advantage is that all their resources are right there: their Rolodex file (for the names of those other contacts you want), any print materials or handouts they might offer, and books on the shelf they think are valuable. There might even be an impromptu offer to briefly introduce you to another colleague down the hall who may have a particular expertise to share.

On the other hand, some experts feel that getting the contact away from their desk and the potential of many interruptions—which will cut into your limited time—is reason enough to try and get them out for coffee and undivided attention. So it's a judgment call. Trying to get them out for lunch is a long shot; it's a bit presumptuous and a big commitment of someone's time. While it's true they do have to eat, they don't necessarily want to kill a whole lunch hour with a stranger who may turn out to be a complete dolt. (Not speaking of you, of course.) So keep your expectations reasonable and stick to your request for twenty or thirty minutes, tops.

At The Interview

You know this, but hear it again: *Be on time!* Contacts may keep you waiting, but you must never do it to them. And be appropriately attired—whether you're meeting in a plush law office or at a construction site. If you're not certain about the company dress code, err on the side of conservatism and leave the nose ring at home. Though this isn't a job interview, you still should project a professional demeanor and show that you're taking your research seriously.

Of course, you will have done plenty of homework before going on even your first interview. You'll have been to the library and looked up recent business articles on the industry and this particular company, and you will have a general awareness of current happenings in the field. You only have a short time with each person, so you shouldn't waste any of it asking for information you could have obtained on your own.

For example, if you are visiting a cable system operator, you shouldn't ask a question like: "How many homes get cable now?" (You could have found that out by checking the annual *Broadcasting & Cable Yearbook,* a staple in most libraries—or even by making a quick call to the National Cable Television Association.) A better question reflecting your preliminary research would be, "I know there's a lot of discussion today about cable companies merging with communications companies. How do you think such developments will affect job opportunities in ad sales at XYZ Cable?"

There are standard questions that show up on virtually every expert's list of suggested queries for information interviews. Depending on the time you have and the chattiness of your contact, you may be able to cover a lot more ground and get increasingly specific, not only to the company but also to the department. After you've done a few interviews, if you find that you rarely get to the end of your question list because of time constraints, at subsequent meetings you might start in the middle or even the end of your list to be sure that you cover all your queries. There's no law that says you must ask everyone the same things in the same order to make valid comparisons.

Indeed, each interview should be considered another layer of information upon which to build. After each one, you should be assessing what you've learned and targeting what else you still need to know. So if in the first five or so interviews you find that everyone basically agrees on a certain issue (e.g., entry-level salary ranges or current educational requirements), you could drop it in favor of covering other material. Go for the answers you haven't been able to find in print resources or the specific concerns or contradictions your research has brought up. And, of course, you'll want to find out whether this job is likely to satisfy your most important work values.

The whole point of your being there is to learn what this career is *really* like, beyond the glossy pictures and upbeat prose in the company's annual report. So be sure to tell your contact that you'd value getting the whole picture—"warts and all"—and that you consider this chat to be confidential.

And by all means, after having gone to all the research effort, time, and trouble to actually talk to this person, be sure you will remember what they have to say. The worst scenario is to sit there nervously watching the clock for your prescribed twenty minutes, worried whether you'll get to all your questions and therefore not actually listening to the answers. Carol Ellin, a career/job search counselor at the Center for Continuing Studies at Goucher College in Baltimore, points out that "you have to be able to hear what this person says, even if it's not what you want to hear. You never know what you're going to get from somebody."

So take a small notebook with you and, as you sit down for the interview, pull it out and tell the contact you'd like to jot down a few notes so you don't miss any valuable advice. It's not likely that they'll object; indeed, sources generally are flattered that you place such importance on what they have to say. If you don't want to miss a single word and you have a microcassette tape recorder, you might even ask if it would be all right to tape the conversation. But be prepared with a notebook in case they say no. Tape recorders can unnerve people and make them more guarded in their discussion—especially when you're asking them what they don't like about the work.

While you're there, you can also catch a few hints about the corporate culture through simple observation. How are employees dressed? Is there an open

▼ ▼ ▼ ▼ ▼ ▼ ▼ ▼

"When you're talking to people, whether in an information interview or asking a friend something about yourself, have it structured and prepared and thought about ahead of time. Know what you want from that person."

CAROL ELLIN
CAREER/JOB SEARCH
COUNSELOR

cubicle layout or does everyone labor behind a closed door? Is there a notice at the coffee stand about the company softball team and a reminder about Joan's baby shower luncheon in the conference room? Do workers have family photos, plants, and personal items on their desks, or is the office decor streamlined and austere? How does it feel just being there?

Questions, Questions

Here is a by-no-means exhaustive list of queries to launch an information interview. Obviously, they can be much more specific or technical, depending on the field.

- What key skills do you think are most important in this work? What personality traits?

- What specific training or experience is required in your job?

- What experiences in college or your previous jobs do you think have been most helpful to you in this field?

- Would you describe a typical day? (If they say "there's no such thing," then ask what they did yesterday.)

- What are some of the lifestyle considerations of this career? How many hours a week do you typically work? How often do you stay after 6 P.M.? Do you take work home? How much travel is regularly involved? Are workers asked to relocate every few years?

- What do you absolutely love about this work?

  What are its rewards for you?

- What are the frustrations? What would you change about it if you could?

- Would you choose this career again? (If there's time, it's always interesting to learn how and why someone got into the field to begin with. What was their education and background? Was theirs a typical career path?)

- What's the most helpful thing someone thinking about getting into this field could do now?

- What trends or developments in your industry do you see on the horizon that aren't yet common knowledge? How do you think they will affect job opportunities in this area?

- What magazines and trade publications would be most helpful for me to read? What trade or professional associations do most people in this field join?

- Can you suggest someone else in this field (preferably at a smaller/bigger company for perspective) who would be helpful for me to talk with as well? May I say you suggested that I call?

In addition, a career switcher might ask:

- How do you think my experience to date will help me in making the change to this field? Should I go back to school?

- What resistance do you think I might face from an employer in this field because of my background? Do you have any suggestions to help me allay such concerns?

- At what level do you think I could enter this field? What salary range might I expect? (Do *not* ask what the contact earns.)

Even if you have not covered all your questions, don't overstay your welcome. If you asked for twenty minutes and minute nineteen has ticked away, make a comment that you realize your time is up and prepare to leave. Even if you and the contact have been getting along so well that you both wonder aloud if you were separated at birth, don't try to extend the time *unless* the contact makes an obviously genuine offer to do so.

▼ ▼ ▼ ▼ ▼ ▼ ▼ ▼

Even if you and the contact have been getting along so well that you both wonder aloud if you were separated at birth, don't extend the time unless the contact offers to do so.

If they say something like, "I have a meeting in fifteen minutes, but we can keep talking until I have to leave," then sit back down and keep pumping the information. But the offer must come from them.

Should you leave a résumé at the end of the interview? Career guides and counselors have varying opinions on this. After all, you're not specifically asking for a job yet; you may not even be sure this is the right field for you. But if you have narrowed your career choice and the contact asks you to leave a résumé in case they think of someone else who might want to talk with you, then leave it.

After the Interview

After your interview, do two things: First, even though you took notes, sit down somewhere shortly after you leave the building and quickly assess your impressions of the interview. (If you did use a tape recorder during the meeting, make your comments to yourself on the same tape.) Especially when you're first starting out, it's helpful to tell yourself what you think went well or didn't. Was there a point where you wanted to bite your tongue or were there questions you forgot to ask? You'll be sure to do better at the next interview.

Second, you will read or hear the following advice a thousand times, yet many networkers will fail to follow it: Write a thank-you note. Even if you backed out of the contact's door blowing kisses and throwing flowers, you need to send a note. The general content should:

- Thank the source again for their willingness to share their valuable time and expertise.

- Mention a particular comment or observation you found helpful.

- Thank them for any referral they gave you and say you'll report back after you've met the contact.

First-Timer Tip: Be a Gracious Guest

When you first meet your contact, don't make negative comments about such things as the directions you were given, the traffic, the temperature in the office, or the receptionist's cluttered desk. (You'd be amazed at what some people consider small talk.) And if you're offered coffee or soda and you don't want either, pass politely. There once was a visitor who was offered coffee and replied, "No thanks, but I'd love some ice water." The interviewer looked startled—apparently nobody had ever turned down free caffeine—and then, to the visitor's embarrassment, proceeded to launch a puzzled search for a glass and ice cubes. Five minutes later, he finally handed the visitor a smudged glass of tepid water, clearly a tad irritated that he'd been made to feel like an ungracious host.

The point may seem petty, but such small things can throw off the whole tone of a meeting. So keep in mind that what you are offered in the way of refreshments—if any—is what they conveniently have on hand. Don't get inventive and ask for a Snapple "Mango Madness"—unless, of course, you are interviewing at the Snapple Beverage Corporation!

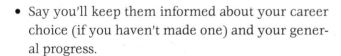

- Say you'll keep them informed about your career choice (if you haven't made one) and your general progress.

Send the note within two days. As they say in the cereal commercial, it's the right thing to do, and smart to boot.

Finally, in the unlikely event that a contact is being uncooperative or even rude during an interview, never respond in kind or cop an attitude yourself. And—this is very hard for some people—try not to take it personally. You never know exactly what is going on in someone's life. Most likely, they are having a very bad day for reasons that have absolutely nothing to do with you. If you feel very uncomfortable, then finish up quickly, thank them for their time, and leave. There are many other names on your list.

Which brings up a question: How many information interviews should you arrange? There is no one-size-fits-all answer. If you are trying to decide among two or three careers, obviously you will go on many more interviews than somebody who has targeted one industry. If you are getting solid verification about a field and your interest in it, maybe just four or five interviews will do the trick. Someone else may want twenty and is willing to put in the time.

Career counselors wryly observe that certain MBTI types could easily research forever until they're satisfied that they've explored the universe. But if you find yourself making a virtual career out of the career research itself, then you need to ask yourself if you may be trying to postpone making any decision at all. Avoid being all networked up with no place to go.

RESOURCES ON NETWORKING

- *Information Interviewing: What It Is and How to Use It in Your Career* by Martha Stoodley, published by Garrett Park Press, 1990

As one reference librarian put it, "I've yet to see something better come along." In this workbook, Stoodley, a career counselor, covers every last detail about the process of obtaining and conducting information interviews, offering sample scripts and upbeat reassurance for both beginners and career changers. Even though the book has been out for five years, the advice is not outdated.

- *How to Use People to Get What You Want and Still Be a 'Nice Guy': A Guide to Networking in the '90s* by Les Garnas, published by Peterson's, 1994

Garnas' book is aimed at people at the managerial level. His approach includes the value of networking in business development as well as career development.

Networking in Cyberspace: A Behind-the-Screen Look

There is a wonderful resource for networking career searchers that virtually eliminates pressure, sweaty palms, and nervous chatter: going online to get advice and information. It can be a lot of fun—not to mention that you don't even have to get dressed up.

The major commercial online services (CompuServe, America Online, Prodigy, GEnie, and Delphi—discussed in detail in chapter 6) all have scores of career-related special interest groups (SIGs). The SIGs are called different names on the various services—GEnie calls them roundtables, CompuServe calls them forums, America Online calls them clubs or forums, Prodigy just calls them boards, and Delphi calls them SIGs, groups, or clubs.

Call them what you will, all SIGs generally offer three elements: the bulletin board, also known as a *message board;* the libraries with hundreds or even thousands of files relevant to that SIG's topic; and "real time" conferences (to be explained later). Whether you're thinking about going into business for yourself or wonder if you'd like working in the corporate culture of a Big 6 accounting firm, you can find the answer on a SIG.

If you are completely new to electronic schmoozing, simply envision the public bulletin board often found outside the village hall or even at the local supermarket. The concept is the same: People put up notices for the public to read and act on if they're interested. The advantageous difference with online message boards is that hundreds or even thousands of people can reply directly to the notice. (You could also think of it as reading everybody else's mail, only, because it's public, nobody minds.)

This is especially terrific for shy or nervous networkers who are intimidated by telephone cold calls, because online, you never feel as though you're imposing on someone. The people who respond to your board query do so because they want to, not because they feel obligated. Another advantage is the mix of people who read the boards—from bicycle messengers to vice presidents of marketing. You may actually be getting very high-level or specialized advice from someone you wouldn't likely be able to reach otherwise.

As sysops observe, SIG members generally are very friendly, conversational, and often passionate about the particular topic and very willing to help someone who asks for advice. The sysops themselves frequently are experts in their particular subject area.

Also, as Janet Attard, the chief sysop of two career-related SIGs on GEnie (WorkPlace and Home Office/ Small Business) observes, "A big part of the appeal of electronic networking is that you're invisible. People feel less vulnerable because they can't see anyone staring them in the face. Online you can be any personality you want to be, and in some ways, that takes away some of the insecurity."

If you're completely new to online messaging, at first you can just *lurk*—which is more or less the online equivalent of eavesdropping. Lurkers read the message boards but rarely if ever post a note themselves. (If you don't post, no one knows you've been there.) While it's understood that lots of people lurk, there's nothing inherently evil about it. Although if you have been getting helpful information on a message board, it would be courteous for you to "unlurk" at some point and offer advice of your own if you can.

The message boards on the major services have their own idiosyncrasies, but their structure is similar: Within a given category or main topic area, someone posts a "seed note" or new subject within that given topic. Others who read the note may then post a reply, and others may respond to that reply or the seed note, and so on. Messages can be posted at any hour and are left on for a specified number of days or until the board's numerical limit has been reached. On a very active board with a hot topic where people have plenty of opinions, a message may "scroll off" in four or five days or stay up for a month. (Messages on some bulletin boards may stay up several months or even years, and then may be filed into the SIG library for future retrieval. This can be very helpful because quite often someone else had the same question as you—and the answer is already there. Files of very common ones are pegged 'FAQ,' for Frequently Asked Questions.)

What kind of messages do career seekers post on bulletin boards or ask during conferences? Anything you'd ask at an information interview, and then some:

- A law school student who hopes to become a court clerk may post a note in the legal SIG, asking practicing attorneys for advice on landing such a coveted position.

- An engineer who has an interview scheduled with a defense contractor may go to an engineering club and ask for tips about what skills these companies are really looking for today.

- A government employee considering a transfer may post a query on a Civil Service bulletin board, asking about morale and productivity in a different department.

- A nervous career switcher may ask on a career change topic how someone else handled going back to school for a degree at the age of forty-two.

- A computer operations manager who is being outplaced may ask for advice on an entrepreneurs forum about setting himself up as a consultant (from noncompetitors in other cities, of course!).

> ▼ ▼ ▼ ▼ ▼ ▼ ▼ ▼
> *As time is money on the commercial services, no one wants to log on and read a message that rivals War and Peace.*

Generally speaking, a bulletin board sysop will set some limits on the length of a message—perhaps no more than fifty lines each—to keep "traffic" moving. As time is money on the commercial services, no one wants to log on and read a message that rivals *War and Peace.*

Networkers should be aware that most SIGs have an "introduce yourself" or "new members" topic, where you are encouraged to share information about yourself, your work experience, and interests. It's smart to take advantage of such an opportunity to let others know you're online. Someone who shares your career interest or lives in your geographical area may see your listing in the new members topic and send you E-mail to say hello. Generally, the career and professional interest SIGs will ask you to use your full name when you post a message, though some forums do allow code names or nicknames to be used.

Your online networking can be highly specific. For example, on America Online, if you want to get advice from art directors in Minneapolis or physical therapists in Houston, you go into the general members' directory and type in those key words—"physical therapists" and "Houston." A list of members who match those criteria will pop up on your screen. You can then contact them by E-mail to make your request for advice. GEnie and CompuServe members also can be searched by occupation or location. (If subscribers are not listed by "interest" in a service's general members' directory, they usually are listed in the smaller directories of the relevant SIGs.) However, being listed in these directories is purely voluntary. The members themselves must take steps to add their names and whatever information they wish to share. As a result, not all SIG members are represented in the directories.

When you join a SIG, there usually will be an announcement about their general rules and usage guidelines, but all share a similar "netiquette":

- *Don't use your caps lock key when you type.* Messages in all capital letters are considered "shouting" and are hard to read as well.

- *Don't use profanity.* Repeat violators will be subject to a *lockout,* meaning they can read notices but will not be unable to reply to any of them.

- *Don't solicit business.* There is sometimes a fine line here, but most boards restrict blatant pitches for products and services. Again, there often is a special library section in which you can describe your business and what you have to offer.

In addition to their message boards and libraries, all SIGs on the major services also offer real-time conferences. As the name suggests, real time is a live conversation via computer. You type a comment, and the various members who are participating in the conference "room" see the note immediately on their computer screens and respond; their replies then appear on your monitor. A conference may occasionally feature a celebrity or well-known guest. For example, on GEnie's Home Office/Small Business Roundtable, guerrilla marketing expert Jay Conrad Levinson was the guest for a lively Q-and-A session one evening.

The Backyard BBS

Finally, the big commercial services are not the only online networking game around. In fact, there may be an active group right in your virtual backyard. Regional and local bulletin board systems—often referred to as *freestanding BBSs*—also can provide valuable contacts. No one knows for sure how many such systems are up and running—60,000 was a mid-1994 estimate—but they're everywhere. They tend to be message-exchange boards only, but more and more are beginning to offer real-time, interactive conferences, too.

Increasingly, many of these regional boards have a national membership. But unlike the commercial services, these BBSs may be free or charge only a minimal annual fee (although there may be toll charges if the BBS is not local). You could start by asking your neighborhood computer retailers if there is a good BBS around and then get the telephone (voice) or modem number. If your town has an active computer users' club, the members will know exactly what's out there. You could also ask the computer science instructors at your local community college or ask at the library.

For a print resource about BBSs, you could pick up a copy of the national magazine *Boardwatch*. Each month it provides a national list of selected BBSs with their voice telephone number and a one-line description of their basic purpose. Many of these BBSs are strictly about computer hardware or software support and the exchange of public domain software (called *shareware*), but others offer a variety of topics related to careers and similar areas, just like the commercial services. For example, a BBS on physics and astronomical sciences is sponsored by the University of Massachusetts Department of (what else?) Physics and Astronomy. It's quite likely that the members of such a board would have a few thoughts on the employment outlook for physics teachers.

Boardwatch also prints the names of "BBS List Keepers," who keep track of boards around the country according to topic category, geographic region, or area code. If no newsstand in your area carries the magazine, contact:

Boardwatch
8500 W. Bowles Ave., Suite 210
Littleton, CO 80123
Subscriptions: 800-933-6038
Editorial department (voice): 303-973-6038

Another magazine that prints a BBS list, along with news and feature stories about the entire online world, is *Online Access.* This magazine is considerably more user friendly for a computer novice than *Boardwatch* and has a glossier style and format:

Online Access
900 N. Franklin, Suite 310
Chicago, IL 60610
Editorial department: 312-573-1700

Yet another excellent source of BBS numbers nationwide (and computer user groups, too) is in *Computer Shopper,* a mammoth monthly publication (it's 10 inches by 12 inches and more than two inches thick) available at many newsstands and in computer or office supply stores. Due to the size of the BBS listing, the magazine publishes half the total list each month, arranged alphabetically by state and area code. So one month you'd find Alabama through Michigan, and the next month, Minnesota through international listings. If you have trouble finding the magazine or want to subscribe (you'll need a big mailbox!), contact:

Computer Shopper
Ziff-Davis Publishing Co.
One Park Avenue, 11th Floor
New York, NY 10016
800-274-6384

Real-Life Online Results

Here's an electronic networking success story: As a law student in California, thirty-four-year-old Terry Carroll often responded to queries posted on CompuServe's Legal Forum. Two lawyers noted his comments and wound up contracting with him to assist on their cases. When Carroll lost his job in computer design and decided to pursue a full-time law career, he put out the word via E-mail that he was looking for work. Within twenty-four hours he had made six contacts and heard about several job openings.

—FROM U.S. NEWS
AND WORLD REPORT
MARCH 28, 1994

First-Timer Tip: Cyberspeak 101

The online world has a language all its own, sometimes called *cyberspeak.* To save time (and thus money) in typing messages and replies online, commonly used expressions often are compressed into acronyms, such as:

BTW—by the way

HTH—hope this helps! (commonly used by advice givers)

FWIW—for what it's worth

IMHO—in my humble opinion

Similarly, little faces called "smileys," emoticons, or cybersigns are unique to online conversation. These are used to show the meaning behind a message when it might be misconstrued. After all, the online "listener" doesn't have the clues of your facial expression or tone of voice to know whether you are being tongue-in-cheek. A smile is made by using a colon, a hyphen and the end parenthesis; a frown with a colon, hyphen, and beginning parenthesis. (To get the effect, you must look at them sideways.)

:-) = smile

:-(= frown

In text, a comment made with a grin is also denoted with the use of the left and right brackets and the letter g:

<g>

So, to you "newbies" (new to the online world), HTH!

Decision Time: Making Sense of Your Research

8

UP TO THIS POINT, your career decision-making process has focused primarily on the stages of self-exploration and occupational exploration. Based on your most promising and interesting career options, you've been going to information interviews to check out those careers and explore them further with the real people who actually have them. And maybe, during one of those interviews with someone who inspired your respect and admiration, you've even had one of those "light bulb moments" when you said to yourself, This is it! I just *know* that this is what I want to be doing!

But, then again, maybe not. No one can guarantee if or when that kind of sense of certainty will arrive. Perhaps two or even three career choices, each of which requires very separate paths of pursuit, may be neck and neck as you finish what you have determined will be the final set of research interviews. If you wanted, you could still go back to the library; you could still go on ten more information interviews. But there comes a time when you have to sit down, put it all in context, and finally make a career decision.

If you are having trouble deciding, you may find it helpful to put pencil to paper once again and weigh the advantages and disadvantages of each career that appeals to you. The Matchmaker Chart on page 137 can help.

Transferring the top three choices of all your self-assessment factors from your Outline for Success on page 58, use this chart to assign numerical values (5 being the highest rating, 1 the lowest) to each work value, functional skill, adaptive skill, life value, and important other factors you choose to list. Next, estimate how high the probability is for each career satisfying that skill or value (again, 5 indicating the most likely to satisfy and 1 indicating the least likely). To get a score, multiply the importance number by the rating—or probability—you gave each career to satisfy that value. Add up the twelve to fifteen scores (the number of scores depends on whether you have filled in the final three important factors) for each career. The "winner," of course, is the career with the highest points.

While this "balance sheet" approach is not foolproof, it can help you see in quantitative terms just how well the careers you're considering generally meet your needs. It may be that one factor that's extremely important to you, such as getting a job that does not require regular or extensive travel, will knock a particular career out of the running.

Sample Matchmaker Chart

In the sample Matchmaker Chart that begins on page 135, here's how Donna, the career changer we met doing her research at the end of chapter 6, filled out her Matchmaker Chart, based on all the information she obtained about each career she's considering, both from print sources and personal interviews. Of her five top-rated factors, she chose the three in each category that she feels are most important to her now.

Matchmaker Chart

Directions: Use your scores from the Outline for Success on page 58 to determine your best career match.

Potential Careers

DECISION FACTORS	IMPORTANCE	Choice #1 Occupational Therapy			Choice #2 Medical Social Work		
		ABILITY TO SATISFY THIS VALUE		SCORE	ABILITY TO SATISFY THIS VALUE		SCORE
Work Values							
Helpfulness	5	X 5	=	25	X 4	=	20
Contact with others	4	X 5	=	20	X 5	=	20
Diversity and change	3	X 5	=	15	X 4	=	12
Functional Skills							
Finding solutions to problems	5	X 5	=	25	X 4	=	20
Counseling or advising people	5	X 4	=	20	X 5	=	25
Evaluating ideas and options	4	X 3	=	12	X 4	=	16
Adaptive Skills							
Achievement oriented	5	X 5	=	25	X 4	=	20
Motivating	5	X 5	=	25	X 3	=	15
Team player	4	X 4	=	16	X 4	=	16

Continue ⟶

DECISION FACTORS	IMPORTANCE	ABILITY TO SATISFY THIS VALUE		SCORE	ABILITY TO SATISFY THIS VALUE		SCORE
Life Values							
Responsibility	4	x 4	=	16	x 5	=	20
Accomplishment	5	x 5	=	25	x 4	=	20
Economic security	4	x 4	=	16	x 3	=	12
Other Considerations							
Good job market	5	x 5	=	25	x 3	=	15
No evening/ weekend work	4	x 5	=	20	x 4	=	16
No travel required	4	x 5	=	20	x 5	=	20
Total points				305			267

Best match   Occupational therapy

Adapted with permission of InfoPlace Counseling Staff.

She ranked her preferred values and skills on a scale of 1 to 5, with 5 being of highest importance. Next, she estimated how high the probability was for satisfying that skill or value in each career (again, 5 indicating most likely to satisfy and 1 the least likely). She then multiplied the importance number she assigned to each factor by each career's ability to satisfy this value (also a number). Remember, the weight assigned to the value will not change; only the number representing each career's ability to satisfy that value will change. Finally, she added the column of scores for each career, arriving at a career that represented the best match.

Matchmaker Chart

Directions: Use your scores from the Outline for Success on page 58 to determine your best career match.

Potential Careers

	IMPORTANCE	Choice #1			Choice #2			Choice #3		
DECISION FACTORS		ABILITY TO SATISFY THIS VALUE		SCORE	ABILITY TO SATISFY THIS VALUE		SCORE	ABILITY TO SATISFY THIS VALUE		SCORE
Work Values										
Work value #1	____	X ____	=	____	X ____	=	____	X ____	=	____
Work value #2	____	X ____	=	____	X ____	=	____	X ____	=	____
Work value #3	____	X ____	=	____	X ____	=	____	X ____	=	____
Functional Skills										
Functional skill #1	____	X ____	=	____	X ____	=	____	X ____	=	____
Functional skill #2	____	X ____	=	____	X ____	=	____	X ____	=	____
Functional Skill #3	____	X ____	=	____	X ____	=	____	X ____	=	____
Adaptive Skills										
Adaptive skill #1	____	X ____	=	____	X ____	=	____	X ____	=	____
Adaptive skill #2	____	X ____	=	____	X ____	=	____	X ____	=	____
Adaptive skill #3	____	X ____	=	____	X ____	=	____	X ____	=	____

Continue ⟶

DECISION FACTORS	IMPORTANCE	ABILITY TO SATISFY THIS VALUE	SCORE	ABILITY TO SATISFY THIS VALUE	SCORE	ABILITY TO SATISFY THIS VALUE	SCORE
Life Values							
Life value #1	_____	X _____	= _____	X _____	= _____	X _____	= _____
Life value #2	_____	X _____	= _____	X _____	= _____	X _____	= _____
Life value #3	_____	X _____	= _____	X _____	= _____	X _____	= _____
Other Considerations							
Other factor #1	_____	X _____	= _____	X _____	= _____	X _____	= _____
Other factor #2	_____	X _____	= _____	X _____	= _____	X _____	= _____
Other factor #3	_____	X _____	= _____	X _____	= _____	X _____	= _____
Total points			_____		_____		_____

Best match _____

As the point totals show, the edge goes to a career in occupational therapy. At this point in her life, Donna thinks this is indeed the best choice for her to pursue.

Now, what about you? Even if your chart points to one career above all the others, you may still feel uneasy about taking the next step. For example, if Donna realizes that she was somehow disappointed with the results and was subconsciously rooting for social work to "win," she should pay attention to that ambivalence. It could be that she—or you—just don't want to commit to making a decision yet, but it could also be a sign that she or you are making a mistake.

Some people call this the "gut factor," others call it being intuitive. Such feelings can be important. They shouldn't control your decision, but they shouldn't be pushed aside, either. If you fill out the chart but feel ambivalent about the results, it might be a good idea for you to put the list aside, come back to it a day later and review whether you have chosen the skills and values that really are most important to you, and whether you feel comfortable with the numerical weights you have given them. You should try to analyze the reasons behind your concerns. What could you do to alleviate them? It may be time for a reality check with a family member or a good friend. Or it may be that this is where you need one-on-one help from a professional who's been through this process many times before.

How Career Counselors Can Help

Professional career counselors have been trained to help you sift through information and options. Of course, they can also provide self-assessment tools and help with job hunting techniques.

Yet many people, especially those who have been in the workforce for some time, often tend to think that deciding on a career is something they should be able to do alone. However, it's also likely that many of these same people think nothing of going to a financial planner when their investment choices seem overwhelming, or seeing a doctor about medical concerns, or consulting a lawyer if they're anxious about a potential legal problem. Well, there are 20,000 occupations out there, and the world of work today is often quite overwhelming. Why does anyone think they should know all about it without a little guidance from a professional?

"I tell people that career counseling is really a process of confusion reduction, self-concept clarification, and decision making," says Elaine M. Sozzi, director of the

> ▼ ▼ ▼ ▼ ▼ ▼ ▼
>
> *"Sometimes people feel a little guilty when they come in and say, 'Well, I know what I don't want, but I'm not sure what I do want!' But that's a good starting point."*
>
> NANCY POOL DIXSON
> CAREER COUNSELOR

Westchester Library System's career and educational counseling service in Elmsford, New York. "Hopefully, at the end their choices have been expanded, they feel more confident in terms of who they are, and they can explain that to other people."

When should you seriously consider going to a career counselor? Some signs that it may be your turn to give career counseling a try: If you've had a string of job disappointments, have ever been terminated from jobs for "personality conflicts," generally feel bored or even rudderless, and still—at 22 or 32 or 42—can't really say what you want to be when you grow up, it's worth getting help from a professional.

Nancy Pool Dixson, director of the Career Center at the University of Denver, observes, "Sometimes people feel a little guilty when they come in and say, 'Well, I know what I don't want, but I'm not sure what I do want!' But that's a good starting point because it's narrowing things down. It's harder to work with people who are interested in *everything*. Then the goal of a career counselor should be to clarify what's important to you and help you come up with the decision that's best for you."

However, that doesn't mean you abdicate all power to the career counselor. "Some people have what I call the 'medical model' in mind when they go to a career counselor," explains counselor Barry Lustig of the Federation Employment and Guidance Service in New York City. "In our society, you go to the doctor, who will test you and diagnose you and prescribe the cure for what ails you. Many people have this impression that the career counselor is the same type of authority who will test them and just tell them 'the answer.' It's a reaction to the complexity of the career decision-making process."

Career counselors don't have "the answer," just good tools to help you reach one. And one thing they certainly *don't* do is find you a job. You should be wary of any who say they will.

Unfortunately, the truth is that anyone can hang out a shingle that says career counselor or career consultant. Forty states have some type of licensure of people in counseling services (such as social workers and psychologists), but there is little regulation of career counselors in particular.

Professional career counselors should not be confused with employment or placement counselors who work at employment agencies or for executive recruiters, whose primary purpose is to serve the agency and client company. Outplacement agency counselors often provide assessment testing and group or individual counseling workshops, but they usually have a contract with the client company to serve dozens or even hundreds of workers losing their jobs. Counseling individual career explorers is typically not their primary function.

A professional career counselor, on the other hand, is hired by you and works for you. They should charge by the hour and be paid after each session. This way, you are in control of the process; you can stop at any time and are not committed to a set number of sessions or months. These career counselors should not charge for an "introductory" interview in which you ask about their services: the types of tests they give, their general approach, their fees, whether group sessions are available, what other resources such as a career library or databases might be available, their professional affiliations, and whether you might call a few previous clients.

What you want to avoid is the type of advance-fee agency or career marketing firm that asks you to sign a contract and pay a hefty fee up front, even before you have your first counseling session. Newly outplaced executives—especially those who left their firms with a large severance check—are often most vulnerable to these situations.

"People who are laid off suddenly or are unemployed get sucked into these contracts because they think it's their only opportunity, and it isn't," says Nancy Pool Dixson. "These people lay out three to five thousand dollars or more—they think they're going to get the magic job because of the firm's 'connections,' but what the contract says is that they're going to get self-assessment. This really concerns me because I often talk to people who have been through that and then they come to us and say, 'I wish I'd come here first.' Our self-assessment package includes four counseling sessions and several tests, including the *Strong* and MBTI inventory, and costs $250. And you can get the same process in any university setting or counselors in private practice. Self-assessment does not have to cost thousands."

One indication that a counselor will follow professional codes of ethics against grandiose guarantees or promises, exorbitant fees, breaches of confidentiality, and has met a certain standard in terms of educational background, knowledge, and competency, is national certification.

The National Board for Certified Counselors (NBCC) is a division of the American Counseling Association (ACA; until recently known as the American Association for Counseling and Development, if you run into older career guides). The NBCC administers the voluntary National Counselor Examination, which is currently used as one of the components for licensure in thirty states. When candidates pass that exam, they may refer to themselves as nationally certified counselors (by using NCC after their names). At that point, they are eligible to apply to be a nationally certified career counselor (NCCC). That designation means that the counselors have:

- Earned a graduate degree in counseling or in a related professional field from a regionally accredited institution
- Completed supervised counseling experience that included career counseling

What Do Career Counselors Do?

If you're still fuzzy about the functions a career counseling specialist can be expected to perform for you, here's the official explanation, courtesy of the National Career Development Association, another division of the ACA:

The services of career counselors differ, depending on competence. Nationally certified career counselors or other professional career counselors help people make decisions and plans related to life and career directions. Their techniques and strategies are tailored to the specific needs of the person seeking help. It is likely that the career counselor will do one or more of the following:

- Conduct individual and group counseling to help you clarify career/life goals

- Administer and interpret tests to assess abilities, interests, and so on, and to identify your career options

- Assign activities to increase awareness of careers and the job market, the "world of work"

- Offer techniques for improving decision-making skills

- Assist in developing individual career plans

- Teach job-hunting strategies and skills

- Assist in developing your résumé

- Help resolve your potential personal conflicts on the job through practice in human relations skills

- Help you integrate your life/work plans and goals

- Provide support if you are experiencing job stress, job loss, and career transition

- Acquired a minimum of three years of full-time career development work experience

- Taken and passed a knowledge-based certification examination

Let Your Fingers Do the Walking

 Here's a sampling of the things you might find in your local Yellow Pages under "Career and Vocational Counseling":

- *Career centers*
- *Counselors*
- *Job training offices*
- *Job rehabilitation services*

Other professional counselors may be trained in one- or two-year, graduate-level counselor preparation programs with a specialty in career counseling, or they may be licensed or certified by national or state professional associations. Of course, none of this is an absolute guarantee of stellar performance from a counselor, but it is an indication that they have put in considerable time and effort and have made a continuing commitment to their practice. (Certification must be renewed after five years and additional requirements must be met again.)

What should you be looking for in a counselor? In his annual guide, *What Color Is Your Parachute,* author Richard N. Bolles lists three things: someone who has a firm grasp of the whole job-hunting process, at its most creative and effective level; someone who is able to clearly communicate that information to you; and someone who has rapport with you.

Where can you find good counselors? Ask for referrals from any friends who went through a career decision process with a career counselor and were satisfied with the counselor's role. A one-on-one session with a counselor in private practice is the most expensive route (fees for individual sessions vary widely, though in an urban area they are likely to range from $65 to $125 an hour). You could ask if the counselor offers group sessions as well, at a lower fee. If you don't have a direct referral, you can look in your local telephone book yellow pages under listings such as "Career and Vocational Counseling."

If there is a college or university nearby, contact their department of continuing education (sometimes called continuing studies or adult education services) and ask about the availability of career guidance services for nonstudents. Most college career centers will provide counseling to alumni, and they may provide it for the general community at a slightly higher fee (perhaps $50 to $65 an hour, but, again, there is much variance). Don't overlook community colleges as a resource; they have many adult students and also may offer counseling services.

Check also with area nonprofit counseling services and social service agencies and women's centers, all of which may set fees on a sliding scale based on income. Increasingly, churches and religious groups such as Catholic Charities Family Services or Jewish Family Services also offer career counseling and support groups. Check in the telephone white pages under the specific agency name if you know it, or in the yellow pages under "Social Service Agencies," "Nonprofit Organizations," or "Social and Human Services."

Large library systems often sponsor career workshops at many of their branches, and these usually are led by professionals. Finally, testing and counseling services are generally available at state employment services (often listed in a telephone book's "blue pages" of state government agencies), though it's likely they will not be as extensive or geared to professionals as the other options.

Richard Bolles also has an appendix in *What Color Is Your Parachute?* listing career counselors, though he stresses that while they have some expertise with the career decision process contained in his books, he does not endorse them.

NBCC will provide referrals of certified counselors in your area. For the relevant list, contact:

National Board for Certified Counselors
3-D Terrace Way
Greensboro, NC 27403
910-547-0607

Another option, primarily for residents in the New York, New Jersey, and Connecticut area, is the two-year-old Women's Resource Center of New York, a nonprofit free "information clearinghouse" of thousands of services and organizations serving women. Their database of women-owned businesses includes career counselors primarily in the New York metropolitan area. However, they do have some national resources as well, including job boards and information for women changing careers or reentering the workforce. For information, contact:

The Women's Resource Center of New York, Inc.
2315 Broadway, Suite 306
New York, NY 10024
212-875-8533

Whether you feel the need to work with a career counselor to make your career choice or arrive at a decision on your own through the exercises in this book and the Matchmaker Chart, at some point you *will* settle on an occupation. Then it will be time to reality test your choice—the subject we turn to next.

Taking a Test Drive: Reality Testing Your Targeted Career

9

YOU CAN READ ABOUT IT, talk to people about it, watch videos about it, but there comes a point when, as the Nike commercial used to say, you have to Just Do It. You have to experience the targeted career for yourself.

You'd never plunk down thousands of dollars for a car without taking it for a test drive. Likewise, you also need to test drive a career, or approximate the experience as closely as you can. Career counselors call this reality testing, and there are a number of ways to go about it.

As author Howard Figler counsels in *The Complete Job Search Handbook,* reality testing is

> any method of personal research in which you can gather data and be involved in the actual work activities at the same time. By doing and observing, you have the unique opportunity to look upon the work as insider and outsider...to sample the wine before opening the bottle.

He adds later, "Reality testing focuses on two key questions: Am I good enough to make it in this field? Is this field what I think it is—will I like it well enough?"

These questions deserve answers. Counselors have files full of clients who earned their degrees and wound up surprised and disappointed by unforeseen aspects of their chosen careers. "The stock exchange had more than a handful of bored lawyers and doctors who took early retirement, and engineers who were dissatisfied with their pay scale," writes author and former stockbroker Laura Pedersen in *The Street-Smart Career Guide*.

Especially if you're considering a professional field that requires considerable time and money for training—such as medicine or veterinary medicine, law, architecture, or engineering—you want to try and get up close and personal to the career to see if it's truly what you think it will be. Obviously, no one will let you try your hand for a day at brain surgery or criminal law, but you can certainly look for varied opportunities to expose yourself to the respective environments.

Certainly, reality testing includes the information interviewing discussed in chapter 7. It is in these face-to-face situations, not in print directories, that you can find out whether the work values and other factors that you've identified as very important to you can be satisfied in this occupation.

But you also need to take the plunge and experience what people have been talking to you about for yourself. For that, your options include internships, temporary work, volunteer work, informal job shadowing, and, if you are in college, cooperative education programs.

Internships

Traditionally, internships are for the short term—perhaps a semester during school or a summer work project. The internship typically is in the student's major; for example, communications, theater arts, or marketing, and is often worth college credit. More often than not, an internship is unpaid, though a small stipend may be offered for living expenses.

Though the focus of many internship programs still is on the "twentysomething" students in their junior and senior years or in graduate school, there are many others that are open to anyone. For older career changers, in particular, an internship often serves to "fill in" a missing part on the job skills list and ease the transition to a new career.

For example, the Center for Continuing Education at Sarah Lawrence College in Bronxville, New York, offers a Career Exploration and Development Program for adults who already have bachelor's degrees. The year-long program is targeted to women who are returning to paid work after caring for young children or those changing professions who are in need of a range of experiences to reach their goals. As part of the program, each participant must find an internship—achieved through a combination of networking and the center's own employment resources files. Each internship is negotiated with the sponsor in terms of schedule, job duties, and pay.

> ▼ ▼ ▼ ▼ ▼ ▼ ▼ ▼
> *The good news is that employers and sponsors of internship programs often may need you—the intern—more than you need them.*

The good news is that employers and sponsors of internship programs often may need you—the intern—more than you need them. Nonprofit organizations, in particular, as well as many arts or government operations, face constant funding cuts and could not function without the unpaid help.

As Carol Ellin, a career/job search counselor at the Center for Continuing Studies at Goucher College in Baltimore, Maryland, notes, "I was visiting an outplacement assistance center, and the first thing they said to me was, 'If you have any interns, we'll be glad to use them,' because they couldn't afford to hire full-time workers. And I hear that a lot. In a world where companies are shorthanded, interns are becoming more valuable."

However, it still can be very competitive to get an internship position, which is why many career seekers go out and create their own. For those who think an internship would be difficult to initiate, JoAnn Kroll, director of career planning and placement services at Bowling Green State University in Ohio, gives this pep talk: "If you were a manager and someone came to you and said, 'I have twenty hours a week I could give you, I have ideas and energy, I'm a self-starter, I don't require much supervision, I'm very interested in what you do, and I'd like to help you'—would you turn them down? All business people have problems they don't have time to get to, so you can create an internship very easily."

To that end, hopeful interns should not think solely in terms of the major corporations that have formal internship programs. It's more likely that your best opportunities, especially to create your own setup, lie with small businesses, which have accounted for the greatest business growth in the early nineties.

If you want to create an internship, start with your network: Ask everyone if they can think of a person or company in your targeted field that might be able to use someone with your skills for a short-term period. Also, contact your college alumni office and ask for their suggestions, even if you're no longer in the area. It's likely that their greatest resources will be in their own region—those are the people they know best—but they should also be able to give you names of alums near you whom you can contact for advice.

Apprenticeships

A few words about apprenticeships. Sometimes they are considered to be internships, though there are a few differences. Traditionally, an apprenticeship is associated with progressive, long-term learning of a specific skill, while an internship is a more general, short-term exposure to a business or profession.

Formal apprenticeship programs overwhelmingly are in the manufacturing and construction trades.

These apprentices are considered employees and always are paid, though at a significantly lower scale than the more experienced journey workers. Many such apprenticeships are sponsored by unions, but, again, on an informal basis, they can be created.

As author Sara D. Gilbert points out in *The Career Training Sourcebook*, "Apprenticeship is required for the skilled trades, and internship is for the sciences, but the systems work equally well for the aspiring photographer who apprentices to a professional, the homemaker reentering the job market who turns volunteer work into a formal internship, or the career changer who gains credentials during a summer's stint at a government agency."

Gilbert notes that apprenticeships currently are growing very rapidly for service occupation workers such as paramedics, computer programmers, health care technicians, bank tellers, commercial designers, and child care workers.

RESOURCES ON INTERNSHIPS

If you are working with a career counselor, she or he can offer suggestions about setting up an internship. For further research on your own, the following are among the many books on the subject available today.

- *Internships 1994: On-the-Job Training Opportunities for Students and Adults,* published by Peterson's, 1994

A staple reference work, this annual guide provides detailed information on more than 30,000 intern opportunities, paid and unpaid, in fields ranging from art galleries to national parks. Listings can be searched through the geographic index or alphabetical company index. Many listings also are open to mid-career or reentry workers. Libraries generally carry this guide.

- *The Princeton Review Student Access Guide to America's Top 100 Internships,* 1995 Edition, by Mark Oldman and Samer Hamadeh, published by Villard Books, 1994

This lively book makes value judgments about 13,000 internships with 100 companies in business, advertising, entertainment, journalism, sports, public service, and other fields. The authors interviewed more than a thousand interns past and present for their assessment of their intern experiences, and only those programs considered "superb" are included. Some pay $1,000 a week, provide free housing, or have the potential for terrific connections. The authors include a "busywork meter" graphic showing the level of menial tasks that may be required, while acknowledging that even the best programs involve some time spent at the copy machine. Many internships are available to career changers of any age.

- *The National Directory of Internships,* edited by Garrett D. Martin and Barbara E. Baker, published by the National Society for Experimental Education, 1993

Published every two years by the National Society for Experiential Education (NSEE), this 600-page guide lists thousands of intern opportunities in eighty-five fields—from dance to criminal justice and fundraising to speech therapy. A helpful element is that you can look for opportunities via three indexes—by location, specific organization, or field of interest. Each entry lists the contact person, application procedure, duties of the position and qualifications required, whether there is compensation and how much, and the academic credit earned. Covering business, government, and nonprofit settings, the listings include opportunities for career changers or those reentering the workforce. This book is often found in large libraries or career centers. It can also be obtained directly from NSEE, 3509 Haworth

Drive, Suite 207, Raleigh, NC 27609-7229. The $26.50 price includes postage and handling.

- *The Career Training Sourcebook: Where To Get Free, Low-Cost and Salaried Job Training* by Sara D. Gilbert, published by McGraw-Hill, 1993

A comprehensive guide to all aspects of learning job skills. A chapter on internships and apprenticeships offers dozens of resources and plenty of encouragement, especially for career changers. For example, the author, at New York University's School of Continuing Education, notes that if someone hedges at sending an application for an internship program by saying, "It's only for students" (read: 20-year-olds), she suggests you reply, "I'm a lifelong learner."

- *Internships: A Directory for Career Finders,* by Sara Dulaney Gilbert, published by ARCO/Macmillan, 1995

Noting the new emphasis on internships, both in classrooms and boardrooms, the author notes that "it's not only students who need to keep learning; it's all of us at any age who want to stay ahead of change." The directory aims to sift out the best internship opportunities in public, private, corporate, government, and non-profit operations and gives detailed listings on nearly a thousand internship sponsors as well as strategies for landing a position. The lists are cross-referenced by career category, location, stipend, and any special status such as ethnicity, gender, and age.

> ▼ ▼ ▼ ▼ ▼ ▼ ▼ ▼
> *Making temp work your day job could help you confirm whether you are suited for the field you have in mind.*

Temporary Work

The usual joking response given when someone declares interest in a career that doesn't seem to suit them is, "Keep your day job." Well, making temp work your day job could help you confirm whether you are suited for the field you have in mind.

Temp work—being sent by an agency to work temporarily at another company—is not just for typists anymore. Although clerical workers still account for nearly half of temp employees, many other workers have entered the temp arena.

As Peggy O'Connell Justice, author of *The Temp Track,* points out, "Engineers, nurses, draftsmen, writers, editors, accountants, bank officers, biochemists, managers, executives, computer programmers, medical technicians, pharmacists, radiologists, salespeople, scientists, lawyers, flight attendants, doctors, pilots, high school principals, paralegals, human resources directors, beauticians and CAD/CAM designers are all working on a temporary basis today, and that's just a sampling of occupations."

Indeed, some temporary or "niche" agencies now specialize in only one field, such as accounting or legal services, or only in management/executive-level people. According to the National Association of Temporary Services (NATS), this segment of professional and high-level workers now comprises 25 percent of the temp workforce. However, some observers feel that media stories about these "elite temps" have given the impression that there are zillions of jobs available. The reality is that an agency may have hundreds of high-level workers in its database, but may place only a dozen or so each month in specialized assignments.

Also, NATS estimates that only 30 percent of temp assignments turn into permanent jobs. That means, of course, that 70 percent do not. But since you are in the reality test mode, these odds shouldn't matter. It will be time well spent if you can verify that you do enjoy the work, even if you can't stay on at that particular workplace.

As with internships, age may sometimes be an advantage for a prospective career changer. As John Artise, a counselor with the Drake Beam Morin outplacement firm in New York City, observes, "There's been a strong depreciation in the education system, and employers worry that today's young people have not been trained as well, so they think, Maybe it's better that we go with a more mature worker."

Temping could also be part of your "Plan B" for a backup career if your first choice does not prove to be feasible because of such factors as finances, the inability to get training, or the need to relocate.

If you hope to find work as a temp in any kind of office situation, keyboarding and computer skills are a must. If you already know how to type well (50 words per minute), some temp agencies will provide computer training, provided you agree to work for them for a period of time. You can learn the in-demand word processing, spreadsheet, and desktop publishing programs. Tutorials (self-paced learning on the computer), coupled with access to someone in the office who is proficient on the programs and can answer your questions, is the most common type of training.

RESOURCES ON TEMPING

- *The Temp Track* by Peggy O'Connell Justice, published by Peterson's, 1994

This thorough, practical guide to the pros and cons of all temporary work includes a chapter on the specialized technical, professional, medical, and legal temps, as well as those who work in science and biotechnology, computers, publishing, and accounting and finance.

- *Directory of Executive Temporary Placement Firms*, published by Kennedy Publications, Templeton Road, Fitzwilliam, New Hampshire 03447, 1994

If you are greatly interested in the higher-level temp route to exploring organizations, you might want to obtain this directory, which lists more than 200 executive placement agencies around the United

States. It might be found at a large library career center, or can be ordered directly at 800-531-0007 for $19 plus $4 shipping.

Finally, if you own a personal computer, be aware that going online could get you additional suggestions and advice about temporary work. As discussed in chapter 6, all the major commercial online services have career-related bulletin boards. For example, GEnie's WorkPlace Bulletin Board has a category topic on temporary employment, and the Home Office/ Small Business Bulletin Board has two topics devoted to the temps called "job shoppers"—generally technical specialists who work on a longer-term, contract basis.

Volunteer Work

Offering your services for nothing has always been noble. If it helps confirm your career choice—or gets you the actual job—it qualifies as brilliant.

"I've heard of people making wonderful connections through volunteer positions—you can learn new skills or get an 'in'," says Elaine M. Sozzi, director of the career and educational counseling service of the Westchester Library System in Elmsford, New York, and a nationally certified career counselor. "Becoming a volunteer in a carefully chosen organization is one of the best ways to help you in your job search—you can network your way to the right people."

As with an internship or temp work, your volunteer experience ideally should complement your targeted career. For example, if you're considering a career in social work, counseling, or psychotherapy, you probably would find it instructive to volunteer on a crisis hotline. The following types of organizations could also be valuable exposure: community centers, family and mental health services, food collection agencies, hospitals, agencies such as United Way and the Salvation Army, or adult day care centers.

Nancy Pool Dixson, director of the Career Center at the University of Denver, observes that "nonprofit agencies are *always* looking for volunteers to help them. For example, if you are interested in marketing, sometimes you can get really high-quality experience as a volunteer for a nonprofit. Then you have some specific experience pointed toward your new direction, whether or not you were paid. You might be able to try this with your church, or wherever you can start some volunteer dabbling in your targeted area."

Also, if you are currently employed but considering a transition, Dixson suggests that there might be opportunities to work on a project basis in a new area at your company, or even to take vacation time and be an informal intern, observing in the department that interests you.

"Management won't pay you to be there, but a lot of times, if they see genuine desire and interest on your part and a willingness to do what it takes to get that experience, many companies will work with you or let you shadow people on the job," Dixson adds.

RESOURCES ON VOLUNTEERING

- *Volunteer USA: A Comprehensive Guide to Worthy Causes That Need You—From AIDS to the Environment to Illiteracy, Where To Find Them and How You Can Help* by Andre Carroll Fawcett, published by Columbine Books, 1991

That subtitle pretty much explains it all.

- *Great Careers: The Fourth of July Guide to Careers, Internships, and Volunteer Opportunities in the Nonprofit Sector* by Devon Smith, published by Garrett Park Press, 1990

If you're interested in doing work that involves, say, improving the environment, helping the homeless, or working toward world peace, there will be food for thought here on both internship and volunteer opportunities. The book generally can be found in libraries, but if you buy it, the author donates all royalties to charitable nonprofit organizations.

- Points of Light Foundation
  1737 H Street, N.W.
  Washington, DC 20006
  202-223-9186

This nonprofit agency can offer information and referrals to 500 volunteer centers around the country. Most are independent, though some may be affiliated with groups such as the United Way. Its Business Outreach Program works with local corporate volunteer councils and a thousand business representatives.

Cooperative Education

You may be able to test your career choice through a cooperative education program, often simply called co-op. However, this method is for those still in college or planning to return, because it is a three-way-partnership among students, schools, and employers.

Some academic institutions use the terms internship and cooperative education interchangeably, and both are forms of what's currently called *experiential education,* or learning by doing. But there are differences. A co-op program usually means alternating work and study, typically with a semester at the company or organization, followed by a semester on campus, though there can be much flexibility in that regard. Unlike interns, co-op students almost always are paid. And the co-op experience is generally more hands-on and directly related to the student's academic or career goals, rather than the broader observation role of many internships. According to the National Commission for Cooperative Education, about 200,000 college students participate in co-op programs each year.

Bowling Green State University's JoAnn Kroll observes that "cooperative education is really big business these days. Increasingly, organizations are developing co-op programs, especially in technical areas and sometimes in liberal arts, because it's a good way for them to supplement their workforce. Companies that have stopped visiting campuses to recruit say, 'Look, we don't need to visit anymore; we can hire everyone we want through our co-op program.' In some industries today—computer science, engineering disciplines—it's the way you get hired."

Obviously, the most suitable source for more information about a co-op program is the college or university you attend or plan to attend. There usually is a specific department just for this purpose, typically titled "Office of Internships and Cooperative Education." Adult students also can contact the university's office of continuing studies for details on what the institution has to offer.

General information on various co-op program types and what should be involved can be obtained from:

National Commission for Cooperative Education
360 Huntington Avenue, 501 ST
Boston, MA 02115-5096
617-373-3770

Job Shadowing

The most informal and least time intensive of the methods discussed here, job shadowing could be considered the next step up from an information interview. Instead of asking for twenty minutes of someone's time to talk about their job, the idea is to spend a day or more actually watching them do it. The more people you can watch, the better assessment you can make.

Again, as with calling people for information interviews, your contacts may be flattered that you want to observe them go about their workday. But keep in mind that since you are asking for much more of their time, and possibly could inconvenience them, some people may hesitate or even feel intimidated.

A lot may depend on the nature of the person's job. Does the worker typically perform tasks alone—say, editing a book manuscript—or in some public forum? Is the setting a college classroom or a research laboratory or a law office?

For example, if you are considering a career in television advertising sales, you might be able to shadow a genial salesperson who takes your presence in stride all day as he calls on clients. When he does have to spend time in the office doing the endless paperwork associated with these jobs, it's likely you could read marketing materials or simply observe the general ambiance of the sales department and other members of the staff. In other words, you probably could blend into his day in a fairly unobtrusive fashion. The same could possibly be said for shadowing a veterinarian, a teacher, or almost any service provider who deals with the public for most or part of their day.

In any event, the place to begin is, again, through networking. You might even go back to your information interviewees and ask, if not to shadow *them,* if they might be able to recommend someone. If you don't have a personal connection, any company large enough to have a public relations department is a candidate for your call to propose a job shadow day.

To that end, however, some counselors feel that the concept of job shadowing works best for the traditional age college graduate who is seeking an entry-level position. They suggest that older career changers who want to try it may feel more comfortable and perhaps less self-conscious setting up a very informal "shadow" with someone already known to them.

Or you might want to find out if a professional organization whose membership is open to novices as well as experienced people in the field offers opportunities for shadowing or mentoring. For example, the San Francisco Bay Area Chapter of the International Interactive Communications Society is beginning a mentoring program, which is designed to match up mentors with other members who want to learn more about their roles or specific skills in the multimedia industry.

Career Profile • Career Profile • Career Profile

Real-Life Results

It could be said that Linda Evans is a living illustration for nearly every chapter in this book.

Evans spent almost fifteen years happily working for a nonprofit educational foundation doing facilitation and training with adults. But when she left to take a similar position in the private sector, it wasn't long before she felt she'd made a mistake. "I'd never run into a situation before where the work was fine but the environment wasn't right," she recalls. "It was just a different culture, and I didn't fit in. I have to say I was shocked, and I went to a career counselor to get some help. Well, the more I worked with him, I realized that career counseling itself would be a very good fit for me."

Evans, forty-seven, had begun her career as a schoolteacher and already had a master's degree, so she looked for a study program that would award her a certificate in career development. Her career counselor highly recommended the program at John F. Kennedy University in Walnut Creek, California. Evans and her family live in Colorado. Enter distance learning.

"I was required to be in California for one on-site session, which I did for two weeks in the summer. Everything else in the program was done by mail, and the instructor and I also talked on the phone and exchanged audiocassettes."

Her studies included a class on how to give and interpret various assessment tools—among them the MBTI inventory and the *Strong*. The students, of course, also took the instruments themselves. Evans had taken the MBTI inventory before on her earlier job, but this was her first exposure to the *Strong*.

"They confirmed what I was trying to do, which was reassuring," Evans says. "The MBTI results remained consistent—I still came out as an ENFJ. And I learned my code on the *Strong* was SAE (Social, Artistic, Enterprising)." As career counseling is a common occupation for ENFJs and SAEs, "It all added a nice confirming touch," she says.

As part of the JFK program, Evans was also going to need an internship, and it was up to her to find it. Enter networking.

"I found out that there were people in Denver who had done the JFK program, so I contacted them and started information interviewing," she explains. "One of the people I spoke with is on staff at the University of Denver's career center. When I talked to him, he mentioned that the career center's director would be interested in having an intern.

"I didn't think I had a very good chance because a lot of people want counseling internships now and I wasn't even a student here. In fact, most of the places I'd called about an internship wouldn't even talk to me because I wasn't part of their university and I didn't have any connections."

Though she now had a "connection," it still took many months before Evans could get an appointment with the director. When they did meet, "I think she was intrigued that I was getting a focus totally in career development," Evans recalls.

Career Profile • *Career Profile* • *Career Profile*

Finally, an internship was arranged: Evans would work at the career center twenty hours a week for six months. That was much more than the JFK program required, but she grabbed it. "I really loved the college environment, and it was worth it to be here while I was doing distance classes, because I was in a vacuum—I didn't have a classroom of people to talk to or any professional colleagues yet."

Evans started out by getting thoroughly familiar with the career center library. Then she began to sit in with a counselor seeing undergraduate clients. For the last three months of her internship, she was counseling students on her own.

Evans completed both her internship and the certificate program in the summer of 1993. She spent a year doing facilitation work again as she looked for a counseling position. Then, a full-time opening came up at the career center and she interviewed for it.

"We already knew the quality of her work and that she fit well into the career center team," says director Nancy Pool Dixson. "So from a group of more than 100 candidates, we hired Linda."

In two years, when she's eligible, Evans plans to take the exam to become a nationally certified career counselor. As the college career center serves the general adult community as well as undergraduates, Evans' work and life experience has been a big plus. "My clients are mainly graduate business students and alumni; a lot of them are career changers and older workers. This field lends itself to someone my age. I definitely think it's been an advantage.

"Sometimes, I pinch myself when I realize that I've been able to satisfy the goals I set when I decided to change careers," she adds. "I really do look forward to coming to work every day."

10

Back to School: How to Find the Right Program

WHEN YOU GET THROUGH the process of self-assessment and occupational exploration, you will, we hope, have decided on your next occupation. If that means a change of career, you may be involved in "retooling by reschooling." Whether you need only a few courses or workshops to update existing skills or you want to go for a whole new degree, you have plenty of options.

As syndicated career columnist and author Joyce Lain Kennedy observes in *The Career Book,* higher education used to be "four square and five-five," meaning it took place in colleges with four walls and adhered to the schedule of two five-month semesters. Not any more. Today it encompasses all of the following:

- Traditional on-site undergraduate and graduate degree programs on a full- or part-time basis at community colleges, colleges, and universities
- Individual for-credit courses in continuing education programs at these institutions
- External degree programs for off-campus learning (degrees awarded by colleges or universities that don't require regular physical attendance)
- Specialized nondegree programs that offer a certificate or other credentials that apply to a specific field of work (such as paralegal training)

- Short-term workshops and seminars in professional and technical areas, often sponsored by trade associations or universities
- Correspondence programs, either by mail using traditional print materials, or "distance learning" via electronic means such as a computer

In *The Career Training Sourcebook,* author Sara D. Gilbert points out that career education and retraining choices today include

> nearly 300 colleges and universities offering special adult education programs; 1,400 community colleges; 2,000 accredited trade and technical schools; almost countless for-profit seminars providing career training; a huge variety of correspondence and distance learning institutions— they're all out there, offering training, degrees, certificates, or hands-on experience in anything and everything you could possibly want to learn.

Nor does additional training have to mean booking it for the long term. Community colleges, in particular, attract many students who are picking up a semester's worth of new skills in a nondegree training program or earning a ten-month certificate. The most popular fields of study for associate degrees at community colleges include business, liberal arts, and allied health professions, but courses in engineering and related subjects such as drafting and robotics also are increasingly in demand. Indeed, even if you already have a four-year college degree, don't overlook what's available at your area community college. Many degreed students are going back for just such specialized or technical training to present themselves in their next career.

Even if you are planning to stay within your current career area, having "fresh" education on your résumé can be a selling point in your favor when it's time for the actual job hunt. It shows you have made an effort to be state-of-the-art, which is especially important in fast-changing fields, and that can help you stand out from other applicants.

In general, adult reentry students should always contact the department of continuing education at colleges and universities to see what's available. These institutions are fully aware of the impact and importance of older students coming back for new skills— one out of every four undergraduate college students is now over thirty-years-old, and at community colleges, the average student is twenty-nine. Many institutions have curricula and schedules designed specifically with adult part-time students in mind, with options such as weekend and evening courses, and sometimes provisions for child care.

Lastly, keep in mind that adult education programs in your local school district also may offer many types of short-term training programs. These are commonly in subject areas such as word processing and spreadsheet programs, foreign languages, or hobby-to-business topics such as antiques appraisal. These courses also are typically held in the evening and last six or eight weeks. Social services agencies such as YMCA-YMHAs and state cooperative extension offices also frequently have various instructional programs of interest to career changers.

At this point, a slight caveat must be offered: It is to be hoped that any education you want to pursue is the result of your goal setting about the work you plan to do. Career counselors point out that returning to school or taking course upon course sometimes masks an attempt to avoid dealing with the job search. So unless you are signing up for a course purely for leisure interest pleasure—which is nice, certainly—be sure it is going to help you achieve your career goal— or, at the very least, serve to help you rule out possibilities as you strive toward that goal.

Still, for experienced workers, in particular, it can seem daunting to return to a structured learning environment after many years, and not everyone is always

Community Colleges Up Close

 Here's a snapshot of what makes up today's community colleges:

- *These two-year institutions are the fastest-growing segment of higher education—most are less than 30 years old*

- *Forty-seven percent of the nation's undergraduates and 49 percent of all first-time freshmen are enrolled at community colleges*

- *About 5.5 million students are enrolled in credit courses; another 5 million in noncredit courses designed for worker training, personal enrichment, and lifelong learning*

- *Women now make up 58 percent of all community college enrollment*

- *The average annual tuition at a community college is $1,275. The average annual tuition at a four-year institution is $4,747.*

—DATA COURTESY OF THE AMERICAN ASSOCIATION OF COMMUNITY COLLEGES.

supportive. To that end, we offer a familiar anecdote. It is sometimes told featuring a different career or starring the opposite gender, and the person may be older or younger, but the concept remains the same:

> A thirty-eight-year-old woman announces to friends and family her long-considered decision: She's decided to quit her job, apply to medical school, and try to realize her dream of becoming a doctor. With the best of intentions, they try to talk her out of it. Virtually everyone belabors the same point: "Diane, you're already thirty-eight— by the time you get out of med school and do your internship and residency, you'll be at least forty-five. Are you really willing to put in all that time!?"
>
> Diane, the confident career changer, replies: "Well, I'm going to be forty-five *anyway*—I might as well be a doctor when I get there!"

Indeed. The only certainty in life is that you *will* grow older, so why not grow as you go?

Career Profile • Career Profile • Career Profile

Mixing Reality With Hope: One Career Changer's Experience

Career counselors often tell clients that the career change process does not happen overnight. Carlo Guadagno's career journey will take many years, and he can't know yet for certain how it will actually turn out.

After spending fifteen years in the music business, Guadagno, a New York City musician, began to accept that his dream of getting a record deal and becoming a rock star was not going to happen.

"I got tired of going through long periods of not making any money," says Guadagno, thirty-nine. "I'll never stop being a musician. I love music, but it's not going to fulfill my material needs."

So he began a gradual process of looking into other areas where a paycheck would be less erratic. "My research was basically talking to people I knew who were doing well, or those who were friends of friends. After about four years, I came to the decision that the only area that's more or less recession proof is something in the health field."

Guadagno started even further behind than many career changers because he first had to earn a bachelor's degree. "I looked through dozens of college catalogs. Because of my hobbies in martial arts and boxing, lifting weights and just generally working out, I decided I wanted to go into chiropractic."

Guadagno spoke first to a lot of chiropractors who were doing very well. "They gave me pretty good information in terms of hooking me up with schools and courses of study to follow. But I think now that they didn't have a realistic view of what's going on currently in terms of entering this field. It's getting flooded. Plus, by the time you get out of graduate school, you're in the hole for a $100,000 school loan. All you can do is start your own business, which means taking out another loan. It's really, really hard."

So he made a Plan B, while retaining his hopes for Plan A. "I found out that if you major in physical therapy, you have a lot more options on where you can work." So he enrolled full time as a pre-physical therapy major at Hunter College and has about two years to go to finish his studies.

Guadagno readily admits, "I'd like to kick myself in the butt" for having avoided as much science and chemistry classes as possible while he was in high school. "I don't know how many times during the course of studying I've said to myself, this is ridiculous, I'll never be able to do all this science, change to something else."

There are financial stresses as well. "To make money right now, I'm just teaching guitar lessons and doing sessions (playing instruments such as synthesizers or drum machines at a recording studio), but that's almost at a standstill. I can make a lot of money one week and nothing the next three.

"My plan—my hope—right now is to go on for a certificate in physical therapy, so I'd be able to work part time and make decent money while I study chiropractic if I still decide I want to do that. My ultimate goal would be a job as a sports team's chiropractor. When I get through physics and organic chemistry and complete my B.S. requirements, I'll see what my grade point average is. That's going to determine what my options are in terms of even being able to apply to different physical therapy programs. I may not have the grades they require."

Which means dealing with yet another reality: Even if he has decent grades, his competition will be fierce. "It's extremely hard to get into schools for physical therapy. Because I don't want to relocate, there are only three schools around here that are interesting to me, and the one I really want accepts 40 out of 1,000 applicants. I have a better shot of hitting Lotto than getting in. So the reality is that even though I don't want to, I may have to move somewhere else for school if I can get in."

In the meantime, finishing his degree takes up most of his time and energy. Through networking, Guadagno was able to set up his own internship. "A friend of mine from my gym opened up his own sports rehabilitation therapy clinic, and now I assist the physical therapist about eight to ten hours a week. The internship is unpaid, but I was real lucky to get this. I'm required to intern at two different places. I'm hoping to do as many hours as I can at the rehab clinic, so by the time I have to do the second place, I'll have enough knowledge to ask for a job."

Of his long-term goals, Guadagno summarizes, "I don't want to ignore the realities, but I'm also very goal oriented. I know what I want, and I'm going to work hard for it. If it turns out that I'm not able to do this or I can't get into a certain school, I'll know it's not because I didn't try my ass off. If I have to do something else in the medical field, I'll deal with it then."

Tools for Finding Schools

The first order of business, as usual, is to head for the library, especially at a college if one is nearby. If you are working with a career counselor, she or he also is likely to have a shelf full of favorite and new sources that would suit your particular situation and educational needs.

In particular, if a public library in your area offers the DISCOVER computerized career guidance system (discussed in chapter 4), you can access information about education programs through the system's "information only" approach. DISCOVER claims to provide "virtually every postsecondary educational opportunity in the United States." The system's files include two-year and four-year colleges and universities, graduate schools, institutions offering external degree programs, and 3,000 vocational/technical schools. The files can be searched for schools that match the factors you prioritize.

Otherwise, the traditional print route has plenty to offer.

RESOURCES ON TRADITIONAL COLLEGE DEGREE PROGRAMS

There are a number of directories of two- and four-year degree programs. This list is not an exhaustive one. Most libraries have some or all of these books, but to get the most up-to-date editions, a visit to your local bookstore may be necessary. Most of these guides cost about $20.

- *Peterson's Guide to Four-Year Colleges 1995* and *Peterson's Guide to Two-Year Colleges 1995,* both published by Peterson's

The first book includes a free disk for IBM-compatible computers, which is a college application planner.

Peterson's college sources also can be accessed online, which offers an effective and time-saving option. If you are a member of CompuServe (discussed in chapter 6) or know someone who is, you can access Peterson's College Database, which contains the descriptions of the two-year and four-year colleges described in its books. If you don't already have the name of a specific school in mind, you can do a search based on the factors that are most important to you, covering 500 characteristics grouped under nineteen categories, including location, entrance difficulty, major, and size.

For example, if you're looking for a university that offers a major in sports medicine, right off the bat your search would reveal that thirty-two institutions fit those criteria. You can broaden or narrow the pool by choosing more features. Then you can display the list of colleges and get an in-depth profile(s) for the ones of greatest interest. The appeal of doing this on CompuServe is that the database is provided as a basic service included in the monthly membership fee, meaning you don't have to pay any extra connect-time charges.

Two Peterson's databases (for graduate school listings as well as undergraduate) are also available on the GEnie commercial online service through Dialog, but there it is a premium service and significant charges do apply for both a search and the retrieval of a college profile.

- *The College Handbook 94,* published by The College Board

If you're a subscriber to America Online, you can also do a search similar to the one described earlier by accessing the "Learning and Reference" Department.

- *The Comparative Guide to American Colleges,* 15th Edition, by James Cass and Max Birnbaum, published by HarperPerennial
- *The Right College,* published by Arco
- *Barron's Profiles of American Colleges,* 19th Edition, published by Barron's

A CD-ROM version of the book produced by Laser Resources, Inc., features color photos of the colleges, the contents of college catalogs, and printable registration applications. It is available for $99 to purchasers of the book.

- *Lovejoy's College Guide,* published by Prentice-Hall

RESOURCES ON GRADUATE SCHOOLS

- *Peterson's Guide to Graduate and Professional Programs, 1994,* published by Peterson's

This set includes six volumes covering the following areas:

Book 1—overview of programs in more than 1,500 accredited schools in the U.S. and Canada, including directories showing which institutions offer degrees in each of more than 300 fields

Book 2—the humanities, arts, and social sciences—lists 10,500 programs

Book 3—the biological and agricultural sciences—lists 4,500 programs

Book 4—the physical sciences and mathematics—lists 2,300 programs

Book 5—engineering and applied sciences—lists 3,500 programs

Book 6—business, education, health, and law—lists 13,000 programs

Other graduate school sources to look up in the library include the following Princeton Review guides published by Villard Books.

- *The Princeton Review Student Access Guide to the Best Business Schools,* 1995 Edition, by Nedda Gilbert

Based on a survey of 12,500 MBA students and other criteria, this annually updated guide to the top seventy business schools (listed alphabetically by state, not by ranked order) includes ranking by academics, faculty, campus life, workload, and other areas. Among the interesting and instructive features are the critiques of fourteen student application essays by admissions officers from top schools. The author has coached business school applicants at Fortune 500 companies and includes some critical questions B-school wanna-bes need to ask themselves before sending in any applications.

- *The Princeton Review Student Access Guide to the Best Law Schools,* 1995 Edition, by Ian Van Tuyl

Ratings for 170 top law schools are based on a survey of nearly 16,500 law school students. The yearly updated guide has comprehensive profiles on each school covering eleven categories, including information on curriculum, admissions process, representations of minorities and women, both in the student body and faculty, and whether there is an option of studying part time. There are even lawyer-bashing jokes, part of a serious discussion on the issue of whether there are already too many lawyers.

- *The Princeton Review Student Access Guide to the Best Medical Schools,* 1995 Edition, by Andrea Nagy

More than 4,000 current medical students were surveyed for this annually updated guide to 123 med schools accredited by the American Medical Association. In addition to student evaluations, the profiles on each school include applications facts and figures, tuition, student demographics, and tips on the all-important admission interviews.

▼ ▼ ▼ ▼ ▼ ▼ ▼ ▼

Nearly 200,000 Americans are currently pursuing a college education in their own home, at their own pace.

Correspondence Study

Today this is also called *independent study* or *home study.* Whatever it's called, it's more popular than ever, as adult students, in particular, who are juggling work and family, find it convenient to take coursework by mail. Nearly 200,000 Americans are currently pursuing a college education in their own home, at their own pace. They can enroll at any time of the year, when it is suitable for them.

There is an utterly amazing array of correspondence courses out there—from advertising to yacht design to zookeeping and nearly everything in between. You can earn a bachelor's, a master's, or even a doctorate degree without leaving the house. Home study courses vary in scope, length, and academic level; some may take just a few weeks to finish, while others may take several years.

Home study isn't for everyone, though. Since no one else is going to pressure you to meet a deadline, you must be highly motivated, self-disciplined enough to set and follow your own study schedule, able to learn on your own, and have good concentration. If you really need the "four walls" environment and face-to-face interaction with the instructor and your classmates, then this may not be the right choice for you.

If you think it is, following are some good sources.

RESOURCES ON INDEPENDENT STUDY

- *The Independent Study Catalog: A Guide to Over 10,000 Continuing Education Correspondence Courses,* Fifth Edition, published by Peterson's

This book describes home study courses at 100 college and universities nationwide, including both degree and noncredit courses. All schools listed have met quality standards set by the National University Continuing Education Association (NUCEA), the major organization devoted to part-time students and continuing higher education. The schools must affirm that their correspondence courses are open to anyone without regard to geographical location, that the courses do not include any on-site attendance requirements, and that credits earned may be transferred to other regionally accredited institutions. Courses are indexed both by subject and institution.

A point of information: This book generally does *not* list vocational correspondence courses. If you are interested in one of those, you can request a free copy of the *Directory of Accredited Home Study Schools.* These are private, proprietary correspondence schools accredited by the National Home Study Council. Send your request for information to:

National Home Study Council
1601 Eighteenth Street, N.W.
Washington, DC 20009

- *Bear's Guide to Earning College Degrees Non-Traditionally,* Eleventh Edition, by John Bear, published by C & B Publishing, 1994

Bear's highly readable book describes hundreds of colleges and universities that offer some type of alternative degree programs and credit-for-life and work experience. Without setting foot in a classroom, even law degrees can be earned through nontraditional programs, and Bear has the best-known guide to them. Program profiles include courses offered evenings and weekends, part-time, off-campus, and during the summer. Bear also "names names" of diploma mills and other education scams and explains the complexities of "accreditation," and why a good school may not have it.

This book is completely revised and updated from his earlier book for Ten Speed Press and is available directly from him by calling 800-835-8535. Yet another version, *College Degrees by Mail,* was published by Ten Speed Press in 1991.

- *Macmillan Guide to Correspondence Study,* Fifth Edition, published by Macmillan Reference Publishing, 1993

The listings in this thorough guide (it's got 706 pages worth) are divided into three sections. The first includes hundreds of colleges and universities whose correspondence course credits can be transferred to formal degree programs, noncredit courses that are professional in nature, and courses that are for career enrichment. The second section includes the privately operated home study schools accredited by the National Home Study Council that offer vocational programs as well as college and professional-level courses. The third section lists the schools operated by nonprofit organizations, private foundations, federal agencies, and the military. Programs can be found through the subject index or by institution name. From locksmithing to business law or film arts to food science, there's a course for it in here.

> ▼ ▼ ▼ ▼ ▼ ▼ ▼ ▼
>
> *Distance learning has been called the hottest education trend of the nineties, and many of these programs have come into existence only in the last five to ten years.*

Distance Learning

Also included under the umbrella of independent study, distance learning programs differ in their system of delivery. As mentioned earlier, you can earn an undergraduate or advanced degree or professional certificate in a course that's "delivered" by satellite transmission, cable and broadcast TV, computer, video, or other electronic means. Such distance learning has been called the hottest education trend of the nineties, and many of these programs have come into existence only in the last five to ten years.

Examples: If you're a teacher, you can earn a postsecondary certificate in special education via closed-circuit television from San Jose State University in California. If you already have a master's degree and are interested in the human services professions, such as ministry, health, counseling, and therapy, you can earn a Ph.D. in integral studies from the California Institute of Integral Studies through the Electronic University Network on the commercial online computer service America Online.

Online study can take a number of forms. Students may download their assignments into their computer, communicate with the instructor via E-mail and bulletin boards, and participate in "real-time computer conferencing" with the instructor and other students.

If this concept sounds intriguing, then check out this book, which so far is the only one of its kind:

- *The Electronic University: A Guide to Distance Learning Programs,* published by Peterson's, 1994

This guide focuses on high-tech delivery of correspondence courses (and thus does not include courses based only on written interaction). It provides complete profiles of degree and certificate programs at nearly 100 colleges and universities around the country and how they are delivered (via cable TV, computer, etc.). Several real-life case studies, predominantly of adult career changers, are included throughout the book. Courses are indexed by both state and subject. This guide, like *The Independent Study Catalog,* also was produced in cooperation with the National University Continuing Education Association.

RESOURCES ON TRAINING

Accrediting Council for Independent Colleges and Schools
750 First Street N.E., Suite 980
Washington, DC 20002-4241
202-336-6780

This nonprofit accrediting agency has listings primarily of independent career schools and institutes. They generally offer traditional business programs such as accounting, business administration, and computer operations, as well as areas such as court reporting, medical assisting, and computer-aided drafting. The council will send you a free list or tell you when you contact them by phone if any accredited programs in your field of interest are available in your area. Credentials offered by the institutions include professional certificates up to master's degrees.

- *The Career Training Sourcebook: Where to Get Free, Low-Cost and Salaried Job Training,* by Sara D. Gilbert, published by McGraw-Hill, 1993

An excellent overview of the many options for adults returning to school is the chapter "Don't Skip School," which includes a list of colleges and universities that offer special programs for older students, as well as sources of financial aid. For other options, the chapter "Success by Association" provides a list of professional and trade associations that offer specialized training programs, some of which can earn academic credit. Gilbert cites a 1991 survey that reported that 90 percent of these associations offer educational courses to their members, while 71 percent offer them to nonmembers.

In any event, the author notes that it would be smart to contact the associations that represent the occupations you're interested in to learn what training and education their members have, and to get referrals to the programs they recommend (if they don't offer training themselves). Gilbert also suggests taking advantage of free training programs that might be available through your current employer.

Seminars and Workshops

Finally, if you are looking for a short-term seminar, workshop, or conference and haven't found what you want by checking directly with a relevant professional or trade association, the following companies can identify sources for you. Both are primarily geared to serving corporate clients, but they will do a search for an individual for a fee.

First Seminar Service
600 Suffolk Street
Lowell, MA 01854-3685
800-321-1990

First Seminar's database includes 100,000 programs available nationwide on subjects ranging from presentation skills to hazardous materials management to international finance to snow removal. Seminars may be half a day or three to four weeks in length and sponsored by colleges, associations, or private companies. The service will research your desired topic and present options, as there usually are multiple seminar offerings. When a program price is more then $500 or involves air travel, the service will provide a cost and quality comparison, then register you for the one you choose. The complete service is $95.

Seminar Clearinghouse International
P. O. Box 1757
St. Paul, MN 55101-0757
800-927-0502

This company keeps track of the content, dates, locations, costs, and lengths of 12,000 seminars. Some of the subjects include communications, computers (robotics, local area networks), finance, general employee development, human resources (performance appraisal, outplacement, affirmative action), management, marketing/sales, production, and technology. An individual search costs $55.

SOURCES OF INSPIRATION

If you do want to go back to school and are worried about whether you can hack it or just fear sticking out in a sea of 18-year-olds, you need an encouraging little push. Try the following titles.

- *College After 30: It's Never Too Late to Get the Degree You Need!* by Sunny and Kim Baker, published by Bob Adams, 1992

This book offers words of wisdom for adult students going back to school, including advice on evaluating schools and programs and doing well once you get there.

- *It's Never Too Late: 150 Men and Women Who Changed Their Careers* by Robert K. Outterbourg, published by Barron's, 1993

Pegged to career changers in their early thirties to mid-fifties, this book features people from many different backgrounds who made significant changes in their work and lifestyles, often taking a cut in pay and status just to be happy on the job. (Except for Tom Clancy; the best-selling fiction writer undoubtedly earns more now than he did as an insurance salesman.) There's a police officer who became a minister, an electrician who became a school teacher, and a research chemist who opened up a bed-and-breakfast. The text also lists resources that can help you learn more about your intended career choice.

Final Thoughts

WELCOME TO THE END OF THIS BOOK — and what we hope will be the successful end of your career decision-making process. The end of that means, of course, a new start: that you have chosen a career and will soon be giving it a reality test or perhaps going back to school or actively beginning the search for a position.

This book was not intended to help you redesign your résumé, write snappy cover letters, finesse tricky questions at a job interview, or negotiate for the best salary. Many good books out there already have done just that, and they can guide you every step of the way in regards to job search strategies and tactics. (A few authors to look for on that front: Richard N. Bolles, Howard E. Figler, Tom Jackson, Joyce Lain Kennedy, Ronald L. Krannich, Robert Wegmann, Peggy Schmidt, and Kathryn and Ross Petras.)

However, we do want to point out one more thing: There actually is a fifth stage to this career decision-making process that we described way back in chapter 1. It's called career management.

From now on, your new and improved self-knowledge will help you to manage your career proactively, which means it is no longer something that happens *to* you but is directed *by* you. Many—if not most—people tend to be passive and simply react to situations in the workplace. They let their organization "plan" their careers for them, and they are the ones most susceptible to unpleasant surprises and negative outcomes.

As career counselor Barry Lustig of FEGS points out, "Managing your career proactively means understanding the corporate culture and your boss' style, setting goals as to where you want to move within the company, constantly networking, gaining visibility, and making sure people know about your accomplishments. Many people still think that if they simply do a good job it will be noticed and rewarded, but often some self-promotion is involved, especially if you work in a highly political climate."

Managing your career also means building on your skills base and always keeping an eye on your next job and what skills you need to develop to be more marketable. And that can happen right where you are: If your company offers in-house training and programs, by all means, take them.

The point is this: When you know who you are and what you can do—when you know you have *choices*—you have a sense of empowerment, and you'll be better equipped to make all of your future job and career decisions. At each new juncture, you can systematically apply the process in this book, considering how the values and preferences that are important to you would be met in any job you consider.

As we said in the introduction to this book, the only thing you can absolutely count on in today's workplace is change. The occupation in demand today may be overwhelmed with workers three years from now, while in a decade, technology may have rendered it obsolete. You'll always need to be ready to reassess.

So if you're going for your first job, congratulations—you're starting out strong. And if you're changing fields, you're especially aware now of the need to keep that skills portfolio packed and ready to go.

Good luck—and great careers—to you all!

About the Author

LINDA PETERSON BEGAN her professional career as a newspaper reporter and feature writer for the Gannett Newspapers in New York. She also has been a senior editor with King Features Syndicate, a member of the articles staff of *Glamour* magazine, and articles editor of *Ladies' Home Journal*. Now a freelance writer and editor, she is currently a columnist and contributing editor to *Arts & Entertainment Monthly*. This is her third career-related book. A native of Cleveland, Ohio, she lives in New York's Westchester County.

WE'D LOVE TO HEAR FROM YOU

If you would like to share your career-finding experience with us, please write us in care of the publisher. Likewise, if you come across information or advice that you think would be of value to others, please pass it along. We may include your story or recommendations in a future edition.

Index